THE UNOFFICIAL
GHIBLI
COOKBOOK

RECIPES FROM THE LEGENDARY STUDIO

THIBAUD VILLANOVA

THE UNOFFICIAL GHIBLI COOKBOOK

RECIPES FROM THE LEGENDARY STUDIO

ジブリ飯のレシピ

PHOTOGRAPHY
NICOLAS LOBBESTAËL

STYLING
JUDITH CLAVEL

ILLUSTRATIONS
BÉRENGÈRE DEMONCY

TITAN BOOKS

Introduction

Finally. We finally find ourselves, you and I, pots and pans in hand, at the foot of a gigantic monument of world pop culture, the work of Studio Ghibli.

If you know me at all, you know the link that unites me to The Legend of Zelda saga. Since childhood, it has been for me a powerful means of escape into a dreamlike and supernatural fantasy. For a long time, I thought that only Zelda could make me dream so much. I was a young adult when I first saw the films of Hayao Miyazaki and Isao Takahata and never before had I been so touched and so moved by cinema.

My Neighbor Totoro, *Spirited Away* and *Princess Mononoke* changed my life; *Porco Rosso*, my vision of the world.

From each of Studio Ghibli's films emerges a tremendous respect for others, a deep rootedness in the earth that binds us to each other, and that also connects us to ourselves.

It's mystical in a way, but imagination is a way for me to escape and look elsewhere. Through the themes they address – childhood, hope for future generations, connection to nature, love, family, the importance of memory, death – the Ghibli films have taught me to look inside myself and think differently about the world. This connection to the self is a fabulous power that invites me to be a better version of myself every day, to be a passionate writer, a husband and a father. I write these words even as Joe Hisaishi's music plays in my headphones and my throat clenches.

This might seem a strange preamble for a cookbook, but if cooking is a form of expression, sharing and creativity, imagine how Ghibli films have shaped my way of cooking and sharing.

Here you are with a book that is the result of 10 years of work and experience: apart from *Grave of the Fireflies*, *The Tale of the Princess Kaguya*, *Ocean Waves* and *The Red Turtle*, I have taken inspiration from all of Studio Ghibli's feature films to date in order to recreate for you the delicious dishes that can be found there.

You can try the pumpkin fish pie and chocolate cake from *Kiki's Delivery Service*, the hambagu from *Pom Poko*, the bentos from Satsuki in *My Neighbor Totoro*, the extra creamy toast from *Arrietty*, the cursed banquet and the nikuman from *Spirited Away*, the shabu-shabu from the Yamada family, the ramen from *Ponyo*, the Tuscan salmon from *Porco Rosso*, and more!
This book is also an opportunity for me to share with you all the respect and love I have for Japanese gastronomy. That's why you will find a lot of advice, photos, and a focus on products and their place in Japanese cuisine. In order to make the recipes, techniques and ingredients accessible, I have given a lot of space to tips and simple explanations. Get ready to discover just how close Japanese cuisine is to ours! I am so happy to finally share this book with you!

I always thought that certain references deserved a special approach, that one should not delve into a pop culture universe unless one is ready to do the maximum to respect it, and especially to respect the communities which identify with it. Having always viewed Studio Ghibli's films as such iconic references. I needed to be ready and in control of a certain form of cooking. Without total commitment, one would end up creating a purely opportunistic book, lacking quality recipes. One would end up creating just another derivative product, with a bland and soulless cover. As you leaf through this book, you will see how committed I am to paying homage to Studio Ghibli.

My team and I have taken on the challenge of creating a true culinary tribute to the films of Studio Ghibli. I hope that we were up to that challenge and that this book, its recipes, photos and artistic direction, will allow you to rediscover with pleasure and delight these masterpieces of animation.

Welcome to The Unofficial Ghibli Cookbook!

Thibaud Villanova

Gastronogeek

Contents

ADVENTURES OF YESTERDAY

ADVENTURES OF TODAY

Imaginary Worlds

Howl's Moving Castle
Calcifer's Breakfast
Fried eggs, grilled bacon
58

Ponyo
Sosuke's Sandwiches
Bacon, salad, cheddar
and Japanese mayonnaise
60

Shio Ramen
Chintan broth, shio tare,
chashu pork and ajitsuke tamago
63

Tales from Earthsea
Tenar's Invigorating Soup
Vegetable soup with Provencal herbs
64

Kiki's Delivery Service
Madame's Pie
Herring and pumpkin pie
66

A Chocolate Cake for Kiki
Double chocolate cake
70

Princess Mononoke
Okayu of Bonze Jiki Bo
Rice, chicken and fresh herb soup
75

Castle in the Sky
Aircraft Curry
Japanese-style beef curry
with vegetables
76

The Cat Returns
Cookies for an Orphan
Butter and lemon shortbread
81

The Secret World of Arrietty
Pod's Creamy Toast
Farmhouse tartine with cheese,
wild mushrooms, and garlic butter
83

A Quiet Meal with Aunt Sadako
Marinated tournedos, steamed
broccoli, noodles and sesame oil
84

The Borrowers' Creamy Stew
Broth and vegetables,
light béchamel sauce
86

Tips

Adventures

My Neighbor Totoro
SATSUKI'S BENTO
SUSHI RICE, FRIED SMELTS, EDAMAME AND UMEBOSHI

LEVEL: *Easy* - SERVES: 4 - PREPARATION TIME: 30 min - COOKING TIME: 30 min

The move to your new home in the country seems to be going well: with your mother in the hospital and your father buried in work, you are happy to cook for your family. There's nothing more enjoyable and precious than sharing a good meal with the people you love.

Ingredients

2 cups (400 g) round rice, japonica or arborio

7 small umeboshi (Japanese pickled plums)

2 ½ cups (400 g) edamame (soya beans) or green peas

8 small smelts or 4 small sardines prepared by your fishmonger

Soy sauce

4 tbsp. sakura denbu (see Tips on page 120)

Salt

Equipment

Pressure cooker or rice cooker

4 bento boxes

1 • Prepare the rice for the bentos: rinse it several times and place it in the bowl of a pressure cooker or rice cooker. Add 1.5 times its volume in water. Cook the rice for 15 minutes, until the water has evaporated completely: it should be well cooked, firm but slightly sticky. Remove it from the cooking bowl with a spatula and place it in a dish. Pit 3 plums and coarsely chop them. Mix them with the hot rice with a wooden spatula and leave the plum rice to cool, covered with a cloth.

2 • Move on to cooking the edamame: bring a pot of salted water to the boil. Prepare a large bowl of ice-cold water. Plunge the edamame into the boiling water for 10 minutes, then remove them with a skimmer and plunge them into the bowl of ice-cold water to stop them from cooking.

Squeeze the pods to recover the beans and set them aside.

3 • It's time to grill the smelts: heat a grill pan or the grill of your barbecue. Brush a thin layer of soy sauce over the fish. Once your grill is hot, place the fish on it and grill for 1½ minutes on each side. Remove and place on a paper towel.

Presentation: spread a bed of rice at the bottom of each bento box. In the center, place 2 grilled smelts, one on top of the other, or 1 sardine. Spread the edamame and 1 tbsp. of sakura denbu evenly in each bento box. Add 1 pickled plum to the rice for the finishing touch. The bentos are ready. You can serve accompanied by spinach salad and miso soup

Only Yesterday
ONION SOBAS
STIR-FRIED SOBA NOODLES WITH ONIONS AND TOFU

LEVEL: *Easy* - SERVES: *4*
PREPARATION TIME: *15 min* - COOKING TIME: *10 min*

Sometimes you remember the taste of the sobas your mother used to make for you when you were a child. You couldn't help but sort through the slices of grilled onions and push them away because you couldn't stand the taste. Perhaps you would prefer their caramelized flavor?

Ingredients

8½ ounces (240 g) fresh soba noodles (60 g/person)
¾ cup (100 g) of edamame
4 spring onions
4 slices of Chinese cabbage, cleaned and rinsed
3½ ounces (100 g) firm tofu
¾ inch (1 cm) fresh ginger
1 tsp. sesame seeds (optional)
1 tsp. nori powder (optional)
Shichimi togarashi
Olive oil

FOR THE YAKISOBA SAUCE
2 tbsp. salted soy sauce
1 tbsp. mirin or rice vinegar or cider vinegar
1 tbsp. homemade ketchup (see Tips page 120)
1 tbsp. Worcestershire sauce
1 tsp. honey

1 • Prepare the yakisoba sauce: in a mixing bowl, pour and mix all the ingredients for the sauce. sauce. Put it to one side.

2 • Begin setting up: remove the seeds from the edamame. Separate the white and green parts of the spring onions: finely chop the white parts and mince the green and set aside. Thinly slice the cabbage and dice the tofu into 5 mm cubes. Peel and finely chop the ginger. Rinse the noodles under cold water and set them aside for a few moments. The setting up is ready, we can now move onto cooking.

2 • Drizzle the olive oil into a wok or large frying pan and heat over high heat.

Add the chopped whites of the onions and the edamame and sauté for 1 minute before lowering the heat to medium and adding the ginger and cabbage. Sauté for another minute before adding the sobas. Mix well and sauté for another 5 minutes before adding the diced tofu. Drizzle with a good amount of yakisoba sauce and mix well! When the mixture is hot and coated with the sauce, place it on the plates of your guests.

Finish off the dressing by adding 1 pinch of shichimi togarashi, nori powder, green onions and sesame seeds to each plate. Enjoy!

Only Yesterday

OISHI PINEAPPLE

PINEAPPLE ROASTED IN SENCHA, VANILLA AND HONEY

LEVEL: *Easy* - SERVES: *4 people* - PREPARATION TIME: *30 min*
INFUSION TIME: *10 min* - COOKING TIME: *1 h*

You will always remember your first pineapple: as a child, you had to wait several days for your mother to learn how to cut it so that you and your family could taste it. While no one thought it was exceptional, you thought it was delicious. Perhaps if it had been cooked, your parents would have enjoyed it even more! Here is a simple recipe with Japanese tea accents...

Ingredients

1 large pineapple
2¾ cup (700 ml) water
1 large pinch of sencha tea

1 vanilla bean
½ cup (100 g) sugar

1 • Prepare the "cooking liquid": the sencha and vanilla tea syrup. Place the tea in an infuser. Bring the water to a simmer and, while off the heat, immerse the tea infuser.

2 • Cut the vanilla bean through the center with the tip of a paring knife and open it up. With the tip of the knife, scrape vanilla beans from the pod. Put the beans in the water with the tea and add the pods. Leave to infuse for 10 minutes.

3 • Remove the tea infuser from the water and add the sugar. Put it back on the heat until the sugar dissolves. Your tea syrup is ready. Put it to one side.

4 • Preheat oven to 356°F (180°C/gas mark 6). Prepare and pare the pineapple: with a slicing knife and a chef's knife, slice the pineapple from the base and to the top, then peel it. Using a peeler or apple corer, remove the core. With the tip of your paring knife, remove the prickly parts of the fruit. Your pineapple is ready to be cooked.

5 • Place it in the center of a small casserole or baking dish and pour the tea syrup over it. Bake for 1 hour and baste regularly. At the end, the pineapple should be melted and caramelized, the liquid well-reduced. Continue cooking in 10-minute increments if the first hour of.cooking is not sufficient.

Presentation: Serve the pineapple slices to your guests on small plates. Serve it with sencha or matcha tea to complement the fruity and herbal notes. Itadakimasu!

Porco Rosso

ANCESTORS' SPAGHETTI AL RAGU

HOMEMADE SPAGHETTI AL RAGÙ

LEVEL: *Easy* - SERVES: *4 people* - PREPARATION TIME: *15 min*
COOKING TIME: *3 h*

Designing and building a combat aircraft requires experience, engineering expertise, and passion. For Piccolo, it's also a very personal story as he employs almost all the women in his very large family! You've rarely been so impressed at the lunch break on a construction site. Here come the ancestors with the meal: delicious pasta al ragù!

Ingredients

1 celery stalk
2 carrots
2 onions
scant ½ cup (100 ml) white wine
scant ¼ cup (50 ml) veal jus
scant 2¼ cup (500 g) organic tomato pulp
⅔ cup (150 g) canned datterini tomatoes
1 pinch of sugar
1 bouquet garni
¼ cup (60 ml) whole milk
Olive oil
Salt, pepper

FOR THE MEAT
8 ¾ ounces (250 g) ground (minced) beef
5¼ ounces (150 g) ground (minced) veal
5¼ ounces (150 g) ground (minced) pork
Salt

FOR THE PASTA
11¼ ounces (320 g) spaghetti
13 ½ cups (3.20 litres) water
2 tbsp (30 g) of coarse grey salt

1 • First prepare the sofrito, the Italian-style aromatic garnish: finely dice the celery, carrots and onions. Set aside.

2 • Finely salt each minced meat separately and mix thoroughly in a mixing bowl. Crumble the filling with your fingertips.

3 • Move on to cooking the sauce: in a large saucepan, pour a good drizzle of olive oil and heat over medium heat. Add the sofrito and season to taste. Brown for 3 to 4 minutes before emptying into a bowl.

4 • Heat the sauté pan over high heat and place the three-meat stuffing on top. Brown it well on all sides for 1 to 2 minutes and deglaze with white wine. Scrape the bottom of the pan with a wooden spatula to prevent sticking.

5 • Stir the vegetables into the meat, then add the veal jus and tomatoes. Add the sugar, mix well and adjust the seasoning to taste. Add the bouquet garni, reduce to a low heat and leave to simmer for 3 hours. Add 4 teaspoons (20 ml) of milk to the sauce every hour.

6 • When your sauce is done cooking, prepare the pasta: pour the water into a large pot, add the salt and bring to the boil. Add the pasta and cook for the time indicated on the package. Remove 2 ladles of cooking water.

Drain the spaghetti 30 seconds to 1 minute before the end of the recommended time and immerse it in the sauce al ragù that has simmered well. Add the 2 ladles of cooking water that you have taken out. Mix so that the pasta soaks up the water and the sauce and finishes cooking inside. Serve hot!

Porco Rosso

ONE-ON-ONE AT THE ADRIANO HOTEL

TUSCAN SALMON WITH GLAZED CARROTS AND CARROT-TOP OIL

LEVEL: *Easy* - SERVES: *4 people*
PREPARATION TIME: *20 min* - COOKING TIME: *25 min*

Many pilots dream of talking to Gina from the Hotel Adriano, or even marrying her. Very few share more than a smile with her. Only you are among her true and oldest friends. You and her go back to the time when you were still human, long before your friends disappeared one after the other. Leave the memories in the past, enjoy a perfectly prepared salmon and raise a glass to Gina and the guys!

Equipment

Cooking thermometer or probe
Hand blender
Greaseproof paper

Ingredients

FOR THE SALMON CONFIT
4 salmon steaks
weighing 5¼ ounces (150 g) each
1 small sprig of fresh or dried thyme
1 sprig of fresh or dried rosemary
1⅔ cups (400 ml) of olive oil
Salt

FOR THE CARROTS AND CARROT TOPS
12 small new carrots and their tops
1 teaspoon of sugar
4 tbsp (20 g) semi-salted butter
scant 1 cup (200 ml) olive or grape seed oil

FOR THE REVISITED TUSCAN SAUCE
2 large handfuls of spinach shoots
8 sun-dried tomatoes
scant ¼ cup (50 ml) dry white wine
scant ¼ cup prepared / ¾ ounce (20 g)
of Parmesan cheese
scant 1 cup (200 ml)
liquid cream
Olive oil
Salt, pepper

TO SERVE
¼ cup (20 g) pine nuts
Baby spinach

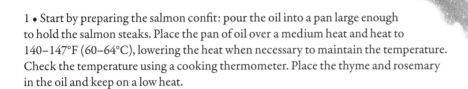

1 • Start by preparing the salmon confit: pour the oil into a pan large enough
to hold the salmon steaks. Place the pan of oil over a medium heat and heat to
140–147°F (60–64°C), lowering the heat when necessary to maintain the temperature.
Check the temperature using a cooking thermometer. Place the thyme and rosemary
in the oil and keep on a low heat.

2 • With the edge of your knife (slicing knife or sole fillet), remove the skin from the
salmon steaks and salt them finely. Immerse them in the oil for 10 to 15 minutes. Use the cooking
thermometer to check their core temperature; it should not exceed 122°F (50°C) so that the core is
pearly, the sign of a perfectly cooked fish. Remove the pan from the heat but do not take the fish out;
let it soak up the flavor of the oil and herbs.

3 • While the carrots are cooking, prepare the oil and glazed carrots: cut the tops off the carrots, leaving
a small amount of stems. Rinse the tops under cold water and dry them quickly. Set aside. Rub or peel
the carrots and place them in a frying pan. Sprinkle them with sugar, add the butter and moisten with
fresh water. Cover the whole pan with a sheet of greaseproof paper, and pierce a hole in the center to
make a chimney. Bring to a simmer and let the carrots glaze until the water is completely absorbed,
about 10 minutes.

4 • Set the carrots aside on a plate covered with a paper towel. Do not wash the pan, you will use it again
in a few moments.

5 • While the carrots are cooking, make an oil from the carrot tops: place the clean tops in a blender,
pour in the vegetable oil and blend until it is oily, green and smooth. Strain the mixture through a sieve
and season with salt and pepper. Set aside.

6 • Finish by preparing the Tuscan cream sauce. Rinse the spinach and chop the sun-dried tomatoes.
Re-using the pan in which you cooked the carrots, drizzle olive oil and heat over a medium heat. Once
the oil is hot, add the chopped tomatoes and spinach shoots, season them finely and sauté them for
3 to 4 minutes. Deglaze with white wine and, with a wooden spatula, unstick from the bottom of the pan.
Once the wine has evaporated, add the Parmesan and the cream. Mix well to obtain a creamy
and fragrant sauce. Check the seasoning and proceed to the dressing.

Presentation: Place the salmon steaks on paper towels and pat them dry to remove excess oil.
Place each salmon on a plate, add the glazed carrots and gently cover with the revisited Tuscan sauce.
Add a few drops of the green oil, sprinkle with pine nuts, garnish with baby spinach and enjoy!
Perfect accompanied with a glass of pomino bianco, chardonnay or pinot bianco!

The Wind Rises
SIBERIAN TWILIGHT CAKE
CASTELLA FILLED WITH YŌKAN

LEVEL: *Medium* - SERVES: *4* - PREPARATION TIME: *30 min*
REST TIME: *5 h approximately* - COOKING TIME: *40 min*

The prototype test did not go well. The road ahead of you is paved with complex problems and challenges. The good thing is that you can learn from your mistakes and improve, especially since Mr. Kurokawa sends you to Germany to prove yourself at Junkers. You return home late, but not without stopping to buy from the old merchant 2 slices of one of your favorite cakes...

Ingredients

FOR THE KASUTERA OR CASTELLA
8 eggs
2¼ cups (450 g) powdered sugar
3 tbsp. liquid honey
⅔ cup (150 ml) hot water
1½ cups (300 g) flour
½ cup (50 g) crystal sugar

FOR THE YŌKAN OF RED BEANS
1 ¾ cups (450 g) soft red azuki bean paste
⅔ cup (150 ml) water
⅓ cup (60 g) sugar
1½ tsp (8 g) agar-agar

Equipment

2 square molds
Baking dish
Whisk or electric mixer
Greaseproof paper
cling film

1 • Preheat the oven to 320°F (160 °C / Gas Mark 3). First prepare the kasutera or castella: break the eggs and separate the whites from the yolks in 2 mixing bowls. With a whisk or an electric mixer, beat the egg whites until they are stiff, adding in the sugar gradually while beating. The egg white should be firm at the end. One by one, add the yolks, while mixing. Place the honey in a bowl and pour in the hot water: dilute it well and add it to the whipped egg mixture. Sift the flour and gently fold it into the egg mixture. Set aside for a few moments.

2 • Line the molds with greaseproof paper. Sprinkle with granulated sugar. Set aside. Strain the kasutera mixture through a sieve and divide the strained mixture between the 2 square molds. Set aside for a few moments.

3 • Line the baking dish with paper towels or a napkin. Place the molds on top. Add warm water until the bottom of the molds is immersed in ¾ inches (2 cm) of water. Bake for 40 minutes.

4 • Remove the cakes from the oven, remove from the molds and let them cool at room temperature for 10 minutes on a rack, so that the steam from the cakes evaporates, but not so much that they dry out. When cool, cover with greaseproof paper and set aside.

5 • Now it's time to prepare the red bean yōkan: pour 2/3 cup (150 ml) water in a saucepan, add the sugar and agar-agar. Heat over medium heat until the sugar and agar dissolve. Then bring to a simmer over a medium heat and add the azuki bean paste. Stir the bean paste into the jelly syrup with a spatula. Continue cooking for 2 minutes while stirring well until smooth. Remove the pan from the heat.

6 • Line one of the molds with greaseproof paper. Place one of the cakes, crust side down, in the mold. Cover it with your homemade yōkan to form an even and regular layer. Place the second cake on top, crust side up.

7 • Cover the mold with clingfilm and leave at room temperature for 5 minutes. Then place it in the refrigerator for at least 4 hours and 30 minutes.

8 • Cut the cake into pieces before eating or storing.

Tip: cut into pieces and wrap in clingfilm so they will keep in the refrigerator for a few days.

MACKEREL FROM THE SUGIYA RESTAURANT

TRADITIONAL MACKEREL WITH MISO AND WHITE RICE

LEVEL: *Easy* - SERVES: 4 - PREPARATION TIME: *15 min* - COOKING TIME: *10 min*

*Honjo is all about the future. He looks only for modernity – for him, the future means progress.
He doesn't see what you see when you look at a simple fishbone. The perfection of its movement,
the beauty of its curve. Maybe it's because you never forget these simple things that you order miso mackerel
all the time when they want you to have tofu pork!*

Ingredients

4 mackerel fillets
3 tbsp. miso paste
2 tbsp. cooking sake
2 tbsp. mirin
Scant 1 cup (200 ml) water

ON THE SIDE
2 cups plus 2 tbsp. (400 g)
pre-cooked japonica rice
Miso soup with tofu

1 • First prepare the broth in which the mackerel will be cooked: place the miso in a large saucepan. Feel free to use a chili miso to add some spice. Add the sake and mirin and whisk the ingredients together until smooth. Pour in the water little by little. Your broth is ready.

2 • Bring the broth to a simmer and then carefully place the fillets skin side down. Cook them gently for 2 minutes before turning them over. Continue cooking over low heat for 4 to 5 minutes. Be careful not to overcook the fish, it is better a little undercooked than overcooked!

3 • Serve immediately: 1 fillet of mackerel per guest. Drizzle with sauce. Serve it with a bowl of white rice and a simple miso soup with tofu. Enjoy!

Pompoko

METAMORPHOSIS HAMBAGU
JAPANESE-STYLE HAMBURGER

LEVEL: *Easy* - SERVES: *4* - PREPARATION TIME: *30 min*
REST TIME: *1h* - COOKING TIME: *10 min*

The Elder Tanuki Council has just met to decide on a battle plan. The elders talked about the great art of transformation, infiltration of the human world, and other intricacies, but a certain kind of fatigue – called laziness – overcame you, and you only managed to concentrate when old Oroku Baba dropped off a big bag of hot, juicy hamburgers…

Ingredients

4 sesame potato buns (see Tips on page 126)
4 slices of cheddar cheese
4 tbsp. homemade ketchup (see Tips page 120)
4 large slices of lettuce
4 slices of green shiso
4 nice slices of pickles or cucumber

FOR THE HAMBAGU STUFFING
(JAPANESE-STYLE CHOPPED STEAKS)
1 large onion
8¾ ounces (250 g) ground (minced) beef
5¼ ounces (150 g) ground (minced) pork
1 egg
1 tsp. (5 g) salt
2 tbsp. of veal stock on ice (see Tips on page 115)
1 tsp. red miso
2 tbsp. panko breadcrumbs
1 tsp. powdered aonori (nori seaweed) or flat parsley
Sesame oil
Vegetable oil (olive or grape seed)

Equipment

Clingfilm

1 • Begin by preparing the hambagu stuffing: peel and chop the onion. Pour a little vegetable oil into a frying pan and heat it up on medium heat. Add the chopped onion and fry for 5 minutes without caramelizing it too much. Set aside.

2 • Make the stuffing by placing the ground beef and pork, egg, salt, veal stock, miso, panko breadcrumbs, nori powder, and onion in a mixing bowl. Mix the ingredients by hand for 2 minutes until it is thick and smooth.

3 • Shape the steaks by hand: separate the stuffing into equal pieces. Lightly oil your hands with a drop of sesame oil and shape the steaks by passing them from hand to hand, as if you were juggling a single ball. This expels any air in the steaks to make sure they don't burst during cooking.

4 • Once the steaks are ready, place them in a dish and wrap them in clingfilm. Set them aside in the refrigerator for 1 hour so that the fats set a little before cooking.

5 • Broil or toast the buns. Then prepare the burgers: pour a good drizzle of vegetable oil into a skillet and heat it over a high heat. Once the pan is hot, place the steaks on top and grill for a good minute per side before lowering the heat to medium. Continue cooking for 4 to 5 minutes, then place a slice of cheddar cheese on top of each steak and cover the pan so that the heat under the cover melts the cheese.

6 • Take the toasted buns, coat them with homemade ketchup and then assemble your burgers in this order, from the bottom to the top: bun, lettuce leaf, steak and melted cheese, shiso leaf, pickles and bun. Enjoy immediately!

Pompoko
YAKITORI!
CHICKEN AND VEGETABLE SKEWERS,
CHICKEN-SKIN CHIPS, YAKITORI SAUCE

LEVEL: *Easy* - SERVES: *4* - PREPARATION TIME: *30 min* - COOKING TIME: *45 to 50 min*

For a tanuki to stay in human form is a real challenge: it has to gather as much energy as possible and stay focused. It's very difficult to stay focused when you're using up a lot of energy and walking past sizzling yakitori. You feel hunger, your mouth waters, the smell of grilled meat rises to your nostrils and then... uh oh!

Ingredients

2¼ pounds (1 kg)
of chicken thighs
1 bunch of spring onions
16 green chili peppers
16 medium-sized brown
shiitakes or button mushrooms
⅔ cup (150 ml) of yakitori sauce
2 tbsp. katsuobushi
(grated dried bonito)
Fleur de sel
Chilli powder

Equipment

Wooden skewers
Basting brush
Greaseproof paper Barbecue
(optional)

1 • Preheat the oven to 338°F (170°C / Gas Mark 3). Place the wooden skewers in a bowl of water for 30 minutes so that they do not burn during cooking.

2 • Prepare the chicken: remove the skin from the thighs and cut into nice, even pieces. Place the skin pieces between 2 sheets of greaseproof paper and flatten them with a rolling pin or the bottom of a pan. Sprinkle fleur de sel and ground chili powder on the skin pieces. Bake for 45 to 50 minutes.

3 • Preheat the grill of your barbecue or leave the oven at the same temperature and continue preparing the skewers: with a paring knife, bone the chicken thighs and slice them into small pieces. Split the chili peppers in half lengthwise and cut into 3 parts. Set aside.

4 • Rinse the onions and chili peppers under water and dry. Remove the green and the root from the spring onions and save for a later recipe, such as a broth. Cut the white of each onion into 3 parts. Set aside.

5 • Remove the stems from the mushrooms. Lightly dampen a paper towel and gently clean each mushroom. Then cut an x in the top of each one.

6 • Put together the skewers, in the following order: several skewers alternating chicken and onion, others with only chicken, only mushrooms, only peppers, or a selection of all ingredients.

7 • Place the vegetable skewers on a rack before putting them in the oven or on the grill. Grill for 15 minutes, turning regularly.

8 • For the chicken skewers, proceed in the same way but for 8 minutes. Turn them over halfway through cooking.

9 • Brush the chicken skewers with yakitori sauce. Then, continue cooking for 3 minutes and turn them over. Coat again and cook for another 3 minutes. Place the skewers on plates.

Presentation: Coat the chicken skewers with yakitori sauce one last time and sprinkle with grated dried bonito. Serve the skewers hot with the chicken-skin chips!

Umi's Bento

White rice, tamagoyaki, sausage and broccolini with soy a

LEVEL: *Medium* - SERVES: *1 bento*
PREPARATION TIME: *15 min* - COOKING TIME: *30 min*

Your friends greet you in class with the day's paper, and it seems that there is a poem about you. No doubt you will talk about it at lunch. There seems to be curry noodles in the canteen, which will delight Nobuko. Yuko will eat her favorite bun and you will eat your home-made bento! As you are about to start eating, you see a lot of students moving about around you, one of them is even about to jump from the roof of the dining hall!

Ingredients

⅕ cup (100 g) of japonica rice already cooked
1 umeboshi (Japanese pickled plums)
2 sprigs of broccolini
2 sprigs of kale
2 tbsp. soy sauce
1 tsp. toasted sesame
1 frankfurter
1 pinch of katsuobushi (grated dried bonito)
1 dash of soy sauce

FOR THE JAPANESE OMELETTE (TAMAGOYAKI)
2 extra-fresh eggs
2 tbsp. water
1 tsp. soy sauce
1 tsp. brown sugar
1 pinch of salt
1 tsp. mirin
1 tsp. cooking sake
1 tbsp. vegetable oil

Equipment

Skimmer

1 • First prepare the omelette: break the eggs into a large bowl and beat them. While whisking, add all the ingredients except for the vegetable oil, which will be used for cooking. The Japanese omelette is sweet and sour and can be served with dashi. The cooking is quite similar to that of pancakes.

Pour the oil in a small frying pan, and use a paper towel to coat the inside. Place the paper towel in a separate dish or bowl, and pour any excess oil from the pan back over the paper towel. Heat the pan over medium heat and pour in ¼ of the omelet mixture. Spread the beaten eggs in a thin, even layer. Prick any air bubbles that might form. Let it cook for a few moments before rolling the resulting crepe on itself. Grease the pan with the paper towel and bring the rolled omelette to the top of your pan. Pour ⅓ of the remaining batter into the pan, lifting the rolled omelet slightly so that the batter goes underneath and serves as a "glue." Continue cooking, pricking the air bubbles and rolling the omelette down again to the bottom of the pan.

2 • Repeat until the omelet mixture is used up. Remove the rolled omelet to a sheet of greaseproof paper and enclose it in the paper.

Set it aside for a few moments and proceed with the preparation of the remaining ingredients.

3 • Move on to cooking the rest of the elements: prepare a bowl of ice-cold water. Bring a large volume of salted water to the boil. Dip the broccolini and kale in the boiling water for 5 minutes before removing with a skimmer. Immediately plunge them into ice-cold water to stop the cooking process. Drain after 5 seconds. Put them in a bowl. Drizzle with soy sauce and sprinkle with toasted sesame seeds. Mix gently and set aside.

4 • Cut the frankfurter in half. Drizzle vegetable oil in a pan or on a grill and heat over a high heat. Place the sausage pieces on top. Mark the pieces and then lower the heat to medium. Then continue cooking for 3 minutes and remove the pieces to a paper towel.

5 • Fill half of the bento with rice and place the umeboshi (pickled plum) in the center. Place the kale on top. Cut the omelet into 3 pieces and add them to the bento with the pieces of sausage. Add the katsuobushi and sprinkle with soy sauce. And that's it!

From Up on Poppy Hill

TEMPURA FROM MATSUZAKI GUEST HOUSE

DOUGHNUTS OF HORSE MACKEREL FROM THE MARKET

LEVEL: *Easy* - SERVES: *4 people* - PREPARATION TIME: *15 min* - COOKING TIME: 2 MIN PER PAN

*You are very fortunate that your granddaughter is so responsible and helpful in running your boarding house.
It is a blessing for everyone to know that she is involved in the community and enjoys the company of the residents.
The loss of her father is weighing on her heart and it is good that she is not alone. With these thoughts,
you can smell the fried fish coming from the kitchen… Umi must still be doing wonders!*

Ingredients

8 headless horse mackerel (or mackerel),
gutted and prepared by your fishmonger
¾ cup (100 g) organic flour
1 whole egg extra-fresh
Scant 1 cup (200 ml)
of water with ice cubes
1 pinch of salt
3 cups (750 ml)
of organic canola (rapeseed) oil
3 cups (750 ml) grape seed oil
Salt

ON THE SIDE
Tsuyu sauce
White rice

Equipment

Tongs

1 • Start by preparing the fish: slit them open and salt finely on each side. Set aside for a few moments.

2 • Prepare a surface covered with paper towels or newspaper. Pour the 2 oils into a high-sided, heavy-bottomed pan. Mix them together and heat to 338°F (170°C). If you can afford it, buy high quality oils for even better frying.

3 • While the oil is heating, prepare the tempura batter: sift the flour and set aside. Break the egg into a bowl and start whisking.

While whisking, pour in the flour. Gradually add the iced water. Your batter is ready when it has the texture of pancake batter.

4 • Once the oil is hot, start cooking: dip the fish in the tempura batter and then in the oil. Cook the fish two by two for 2 min, then remove with tongs onto paper towels.

Serve these horse mackerel tempuras immediately while they are still crispy! Serve with tsuyu sauce and white rice. Enjoy!

Adventures

My neighbors the Yamadas
WINTER SHABU-SHABU FROM MATSUKO
KOMBU BROTH AND VEGETABLE FONDUE

LEVEL: *Easy* - SERVES: *4* - PREPARATION TIME: *20 min* - REST TIME: *20 min* - COOKING TIME: *Continuous*

Matsuko could tell you that there is nothing better than a good nabemono, a fondue or stew, to warm up the body and the soul in winter! Shige, her mother-in-law, would tell you that it's especially convenient when you don't feel like cooking!

Ingredients

14 ounces (400 g) sirloin steak
2 leeks
8 shiitakes
1 small bunch of shimeji mushrooms
13¼ cups (400 g) fresh spinach
¾ cup (200 g) napa (Chinese) cabbage
8½ ounces (240 g) firm tofu
1 scant cup (150 g) rice vermicelli
Ponzu sauce

FOR THE BROTH
8½ cups (2 litres) of water
1 piece of kombu seaweed
2 tbsp. soy sauce
1 tbsp. mirin

Equipment

Fondue maker or slow cooker
Casserole dish

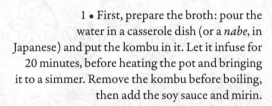

1 • First, prepare the broth: pour the water in a casserole dish (or a *nabe*, in Japanese) and put the kombu in it. Let it infuse for 20 minutes, before heating the pot and bringing it to a simmer. Remove the kombu before boiling, then add the soy sauce and mirin.

2 • Put the steak in the freezer for 15 minutes to firm it up and allow you to cut extra-thin slices.

3 • While the broth is brewing, prepare the vegetables: rinse them all except the mushrooms, which you can clean gently with a dampened paper towel. Remove the green and the roots from the leeks. Place them in a container in the refrigerator for later use, such as in a broth. Cut the whites of the leeks into chunks. Cut the cabbage leaves in half. Cut the tofu into thick slices. Chop the meat as finely as possible.

4 • Now arrange the vegetables and mushrooms: place the tofu, vermicelli rice and meat on small plates on the table. In the middle of the table, place a stove, light it and put the broth pot on it.

5 • Place the ingredients in the broth to cook. Leave the vermicelli rice in the broth for 2 to 3 minutes before eating it. Put the meat slices in the broth for about 20 seconds to cook them. Shabu-shabu is the name of the dish but also the sound that the meat makes when it cooks in the broth!

Enjoy the vegetables, meat and vermicelli rice at your convenience. Let the broth take on the flavors of your ingredients. Use ponzu sauce to season the cooked ingredients of this shabu-shabu. *Itadakimasu!*

Tip: To make this dish vegetarian, simply remove the meat.

My Neighbors the Yamadas
YAMADA BITES
GYOZAS AND HOMEMADE KOROKKE

Three generations living under the same roof is not always easy to manage! We don't always have the opportunity to prepare a variety of dishes, but sometimes inspiration comes and we get caught up in cooking specialties that are easy to share!

THE GYOZAS

LEVEL: *Medium* - SERVES: *4* - PREPARATION TIME: *20 min* - REST TIME: *30 min* - COOKING TIME: *10 min*

Ingredients

16 to 20 discs of gyoza dough
Flour for the work surface
Sesame oil
2 tbsp. neutral vegetable oil for cooking (sunflower or grape seed)
Salt, pepper

FOR THE STUFFING OF GYOZAS
1 clove of garlic
¾ inch (1 cm) fresh ginger
1 small leek
¼ cup of napa (Chinese) cabbage
5¼ ounces (150 g) raw shrimp
5¼ ounces (150 g) ground (minced) pork
1 tsp. potato starch
3 tsp. soy sauce soup
1 tsp. sake
1 tsp. sesame oil

Equipment

Mixer
Skimmer or frying spider

1 • Start by preparing the gyoza filling: peel and crush the garlic and ginger. Rinse the leek under fresh water, remove the stale parts and the root. Chop coarsely. Rinse the cabbage and do the same. Set aside. Prepare the shrimp: peel and gut them (remove the black filament on the back of the shrimp, these are its intestines). Cut the shrimp into large pieces.

2 • Place all these ingredients in a blender. Blend for 1 to 2 minutes in quick succession to incorporate all ingredients and obtain a smooth texture.

3 • Put the stuffing in a bowl and add the pork, potato starch, soy sauce, sake and sesame oil. Mix the stuffing thoroughly with your hands, then wrap in clingfilm and keep it in a cool place for 30 minutes.

4 • Take the stuffing and the gyozas: lightly flour the work surface and a dish. Place the discs of dough on the work surface and shape the gyozas: coat the edges of the discs with a little water and place a portion of filling in the center of the disc. Close the dough in on itself, pressing the edges together. Place the first gyoza in the lightly floured dish and continue until all the ingredients are used up. Tip: At this point, you can freeze the gyozas for later use.

5 • Move on to cooking: pour the vegetable oil into the bottom of a pan. Heat over high heat and, once the oil is hot, fry the gyozas for 2 minutes before adding 4 tbsp. of water, lowering the heat to medium and covering the pan. Continue cooking for another 2 to 3 minutes with the pan covered. Finally, uncover the pan, drizzle with sesame oil and continue cooking for 1 minute before removing to a cooling rack.

Tip: Serve with salad and a small bowl of black vinegar.

THE KOROKKE

LEVEL: *Medium* - SERVES: *4* - PREPARATION TIME: *20 min* - COOKING TIME: *35 min*

Ingredients

4 large mashed potatoes
½ tsp. (20 g) coarse salt
1 spring onion
½ bunch flat-leaf parsley
5¼ ounces (150 g) ground (minced) beef
1 tsp. soy sauce

2 eggs
10 tbsp. (80 g) potato starch or flour
1¾ cups (140 g) panko breadcrumbs
6⅓ cups (1.5 litres) frying oil
Salt, pepper

Equipment

Potato masher (optional)
Cooking thermometer or probe
Skimmer or frying spider

1 • Start by preparing the potatoes: rinse under water before placing them in a large pot. It is better not to peel them before cooking, keeping the skin will give them a more authentic taste. Cover with 8½ cups (2 litres) of cold water, add coarse salt and bring to the boil. Continue cooking for 20 minutes until the potatoes have cooked through.

2 • While they are cooking, prepare the stuffing: rinse the spring onion, cut the root and remove the stale parts. Chop the green and white parts. Chop the flat-leaf parsley. Place the onion, parsley, ground beef and soy sauce in a bowl and mix well. Set aside.

3 • Drain the potatoes and peel them with a paring knife. You can run them under cold water for a few moments so you can handle them without burning yourself. Then mash the potato with a potato masher or a fork to make a thick purée. Then stir the previously cooked stuffing into the potato.

4 • Prepare the breadcrumbs: in one bowl, break the eggs, salt lightly and beat them into an omelette; in another bowl, pour in the starch or flour; in a final bowl, pour in the panko breadcrumbs.

5 • Pour the oil into a saucepan and bring it to 338°F (170°C). Check the temperature with a probe or a cooking thermometer. Prepare a flat surface covered with paper towels.

6 • In the meantime, flour your hands and take the equivalent of 2 tbsp. of korokke mixture. Between your palms, shape a ball, coat it with flour and then dip it in the beaten egg, then in the breadcrumbs, again in the egg and a last time in the breadcrumbs to create a nice crust. This way, the balls will not fall apart when cooked.

7 • Once your first ball is ready, place it on a plate and make the others. Once the oil is hot, immerse the balls in the oil for 2 minutes each, until they are a nice golden color. Using a skimmer or spider, remove the cooked korokke from the oil and immediately place them on the paper towels. Use other paper towels to pat the balls and absorb as much of the oil as possible.

Tip: Serve your delicious korokke with fresh, crisp salad leaves. They are also great with hot sauce!

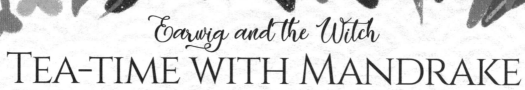

Earwig and the Witch
TEA-TIME WITH MANDRAKE
ENGLISH-STYLE CHERRY COOKIES AND CUPCAKES

Considering his usual behavior, you didn't expect to see Mandrake and a tray of cookies appear in the workshop where you were working with Thomas. Not a word, not an answer to your questions, just a dark look, a tray and some very yummy treats!

THE BISCUITS

LEVEL: *Easy* - SERVES: *16 cookies* - PREPARATION TIME: *10 min* - BAKING TIME: *15 min*

Ingredients

1 sachet vanilla sugar
1 egg
Scant ½ cup (100 ml) milk
1⅔ cups (200 g) flour
⅓ cup plus 1 tbsp. (50 g) hazelnut powder
1 packet baking powder
1 jar of candied cherries

FOR THE ROYAL ICING
1 cup (200 g) powdered sugar
1 egg white
The juice of ½ lemon

Equipment

Rubber spatula (maryse)
Rolling pin
2-inch (5-cm) diameter cookie cutter
Greaseproof paper

1 • Preheat the oven to 356°F (180 °C / Gas Mark 4). Prepare the cookie mixture: cut the butter into pieces and place in a bowl. Using a blender, stir the sugars into the butter until smooth. Whisk in the egg and milk. Finally, add the flour, hazelnut powder and baking powder until you have a smooth dough.

2 • Lightly flour the work surface and roll out the dough 2 mm thick. Cut out the dough with a cookie cutter to make 16 cookies. Place all the cookies on a baking sheet lined with greaseproof paper and bake for 15 minutes.

3 • Take the cookies out of the oven as soon as they look firm and start to turn golden brown. Let them cool on a wire rack and decorate them when they have cooled completely.

4 • Move on to the preparation of the royal icing: put the powdered sugar in a bowl. Add the egg white and mix until smooth. Pour in the lemon juice and mix until smooth and shiny. Your royal icing is ready!

Decorate the cookies with the royal icing and place 1 candied cherry in the center of each.

THE CUPCAKES

LEVEL: *Easy* - SERVES: *16 cupcakes* - PREPARATION TIME: *20 min* - COOKING TIME: *10 min*

Ingredients

½ cup (100 g) sugar
4 eggs
¾ cup (100 g) flour
1 sachet of yeast
½ cup (135 g) melted butter
1½ cup (300 g) mascarpone cheese
¼ cup (50 g) of powdered sugar
2 drops of red food coloring
2 drops of green food coloring

Equipment

16 small cardboard or silicone cupcake molds
2 piping bags and 2 fluted piping bags

1 • Preheat oven to 356°F (180°C / gas mark 4). Prepare the cupcake mix: in a large bowl, pour the sugar and eggs. Whisk until smooth and light. Add the flour and baking powder and mix well. Add in the melted butter with the help of a spatula or whisk. Pour the mixture into the molds and bake for 15 minutes.

2 • While baking, prepare the mascarpone glaze: separate the mascarpone and powdered sugar into two bowls.

Whisk until the well combined.

3 • Add the red coloring to one bowl and the green coloring to the other bowl. Mix and place each colored whipped cream in a piping bag. Set aside in a cool spot.

Presentation: once the cupcakes are out of the oven and have cooled, use the piping bags to add the mascarpone frosting and enjoy! Perfect with a nice cup of tea and a splash of milk.

Earwig and the Witch
SHEPHERD'S PIE FROM THE ORPH
SHEPHERD'S PIE WITH TOMATO

LEVEL: *Easy* - SERVES: *4* - PREPARATION TIME: *15 min* - COOKING TIME: *1 h*

Magic is mysterious, strange, and sometimes terrifying. Just like Mandrake and Bella Yaga, after all! It can be used for many purposes, to manipulate the supernatural, to make potions... Speaking of Mandrake, it's curious that your favorite dish is also hers: a good shepherd's pie with tomato, like the one they served you at the orphanage. Isn't that something?

Ingredients

FOR THE MASHED POTATOES
1½ pounds (600 g) potatoes (Ratte or Charlotte)
¾ cup (175 g) soft butter
Scant 1 cup (200 ml) whole milk
Nutmeg
Coarse salt, fleur de sel, pepper

FOR THE STUFFING
1 onion
2 shallots
2 carrots
1 stick of celery
¾ cup (100 g) of peas
½ bunch parsley 5¼ ounces (150 g) ground (minced) beef
12¼ ounces (350 g) ground (minced) lamb
Flour

Scant ½ cup (100 ml) red wine
⅔ cup (150 ml) of veal stock (see Tips page 117)
2 tbsp. Worcestershire sauce
Scant ½ cup (100 ml) canned crushed tomatoes
1 pinch of sugar
1 tbsp. dried thyme
1 tbsp. dried rosemary
Sunflower oil
Salt, pepper

Equipment

Potato masher piping bag
and fluted piping bag
Baking dish

1 • First prepare the mashed potatoes: rinse the potatoes but do not peel them. Place them in a large pot filled with cold water. Add 2 tsp. (10 g) of coarse salt per liter of water. Bring to a boil and cook for 20 to 25 minutes, until the potatoes are melting in the middle. Peel them and mash with a potato masher.

2 • Dice the cold butter and bring the milk to a simmer in a saucepan. Place the potato pulp in a saucepan and heat over medium heat, stirring constantly with a wooden spatula, for 2 min, until dry. Remove the pan from the heat. Gradually add the cold butter. Do the same with the simmering milk. Once the mixture is smooth, the purée is ready. Put it in a piping bag and set aside for a few moments.

3 • Preheat oven to 356°F (180°C / gas mark 4). Prepare the stuffing: peel and finely chop the onion and shallots. Peel the carrots and dice finely (brunoise). Do the same with the celery. Rinse the peas. Chop the parsley finely. In a bowl, salt and mix the two meats thoroughly.

4 • Next, drizzle sunflower oil into a frying pan and heat over a medium heat. Place the onion, shallots, celery and carrots in the hot oil. Season with salt and pepper. Brown the vegetables for 2 to 3 minutes before removing them from the pan. Put the pan on high heat and, once it is hot, brown the meat for 2 minutes on each side, then separate into chunks with a wooden spatula. Sprinkle the meat with a little flour, deglaze with red wine and mix well. Continue cooking until the wine evaporates.

5 • Mix the vegetables back in, add the peas, then the veal stock and Worcestershire sauce. Add the crushed tomatoes, the pinch of sugar, the thyme, the rosemary and mix well. Check the seasonings and adjust to taste. Continue cooking for 20 minutes over medium heat, with the pan covered.

6 • Butter the dish and pour in the stuffing and the vegetables. Put the mashed potatoes on top using the piping bags and bake for 30 minutes. Serve hot.

Whisper of the Heart

TAMAGO KAKE GOHAN FROM SHIZUKU

RICE, RAW EGG, SOY SAUCE AND HOMEMADE FURIKAKE POWDER

LEVEL: *Easy* - SERVES: *4 bowls* - PREPARATION TIME: *10 min* - REST TIME: *30 min*
COOKING TIME: *20 min*

You have only just woken up when your sister gives you a ton of chores to do. You barely have time to finish your tamago kake gohan because there are so many orders; then you have to bring your father's lunch to him, he left for work without it! Who knows, maybe there is an adventure waiting for you on the horizon...

Ingredients

2 cups (360 g) of japonica rice
1⅔ cups (400 ml) water
4 organic eggs extra-fresh
4 tbsp. soy sauce

FOR FURIKAKE POWDER
1 tsp. fleur de sel
1 tsp. roasted sesame seeds
1 tsp. nori powder
or nori leaf flakes
1 pinch of katsuobushi

Equipment

Rice cooker (if possible)
Blender or mortar

1 • Prepare the rice in the cooker: rinse the rice with clear, cold water 3 times before placing it in the removable bowl of the cooker. Pour in the water. Let the rice rest in the water for 30 minutes before turning on the machine. Let the rice cook until the machine indicates that it is ready.

2 • Meanwhile, prepare the furikake powder: in the bowl of a blender or in a mortar, place all the ingredients. Blend them coarsely or crush them with a pestle for a few moments, to achieve a smooth mixture. Set aside.

3 • Once the rice is cooked and hot, divide it among the bowls. Make a small well in the center of each bowl of rice and break into it 1 egg. Add 1 tbsp. of soy sauce per bowl and mix well. Let it stand for 1 to 2 minutes until the egg cooks thanks to the heat of the rice.

Presentation: sprinkle each bowl with your homemade furikake powder (and save the rest for later use). Serve with a small bowl of hot miso soup. This is a typical and delicious Japanese breakfast!

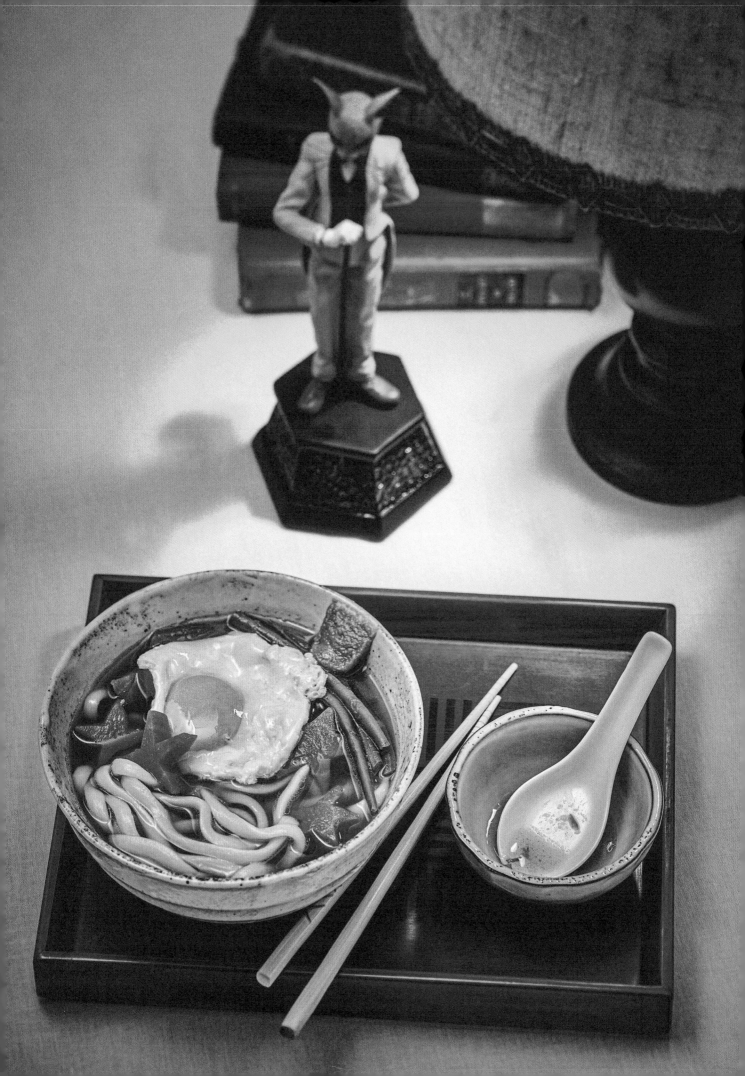

Whisper of the Heart
WARMING WINTER SOUP
DASHI BROTH, FRIED EGG, VEGETABLES AND UDON

LEVEL: *Medium* - SERVES: *4 bowls* - PREPARATION TIME: *10 min* - COOKING TIME: *45 min*

At last you have confessed your love for Seiji to someone, you have opened your heart and told your story. You are overcome with emotion and you suddenly burst into tears. Fortunately, the kind Mr. Nishi welcomes you and offers you a comforting soup to calm your nerves...

Ingredients

8½ cups (2 litres) of dashi broth (see Tips page 114)
⅔ cup (100 g) canned organic green beans
1 clove of garlic
1½ inches (2 cm) fresh ginger
4 spring onions
2 carrots

2 large dried shiitakes
3 tbsp. soy sauce
1 tbsp. mirin
14 ounces (400 g) wheat noodles (udon)
4 eggs
Sesame oil
Vegetable cooking oil

Equipment

Small star-shaped cookie cutter (optional)

1 • First, prepare the base of your soup: pour the dashi broth into a large pot and bring it to a simmer.

2 • Prepare the vegetables: Drain and rinse the green beans. Set them aside. Peel and chop the garlic and ginger. Add them to the broth. Rinse the new onions. Remove the roots and stale parts and then separate the white from the green parts. Thinly slice the green parts and slice the onions in half. Add to the broth. Rinse the carrots and cut them into thick slices. Using a star-shaped cookie cutter or a paring knife, cut out stars from the carrot slices. Place the carrot stars and remaining trimmings in the broth.

3 • Finally, add the mushrooms, soy sauce and mirin and mix. Let it simmer, covered, for 35 to 40 minutes.

4 • Bring a large volume of water to a boil and cook the noodles for 7 minutes.

5 • In the meantime, pour a good drizzle of oil into a frying pan and place over medium heat: once the oil is hot, break the eggs into the pan and cook them until the whites begin to solidify. Remove the eggs to a plate and separate them.

6 • Take a ladleful of cooking water from the noodles and then drain. Put them back in their pot and drizzle with a thin layer of sesame oil and the cooking water. Separate the noodles so that they do not stick together and proceed to dressing.

Presentation: Divide the noodles into 4 large bowls and fill with broth. Garnish each bowl with the carrot stars, spring onions, green beans and fried egg.
Enjoy!

When Marnie Was There
DAWN PICNIC
JAM-FILLED COOKIES

LEVEL: *Easy* - SERVES: *16 cookies* - PREPARATION TIME: *15 min* - COOKING TIME: *10 min*

You feel a strange and deep connection with Marnie and the Marshes villa. There is something about this girl that feels familiar and makes you want to open up to her. In her company, the world seems easier to face. Here she comes in a boat, a picnic basket at her side...

Ingredients

⅔ cup (150 g) soft butter, at room temperature
½ cup (100 g) powdered sugar
1⅓ cups (200 g) flour + flour to work the dough
⅓ cup (40 g) almond powder
1 pinch of salt
3 tbsp. strawberry jam

Equipment

Flexible spatula
Greaseproof paper

1 • Preheat oven to 356°F (180°C / gas mark 4). Prepare the cookie mix: cut the butter into pieces and place in a bowl. Using a flexible spatula, work the butter to make it creamy and, while doing so, incorporate the powdered sugar. Mix until smooth. Sift the flour and almond powder and add them to the sweet butter mixture. Season with salt.

2 • Line a baking sheet with greaseproof paper. Flour your hands before making the cookies: scoop out about a tablespoon of dough. Work the dough between your palms and fingertips to make a small ball. Press the center of this ball of dough to make a small well and put a touch of jam inside. Place the cookie on the baking sheet. Continue until the dough is used up, then bake the cookies for 10 minutes.

3 • Remove the cookies from the oven and place them on a rack to cool.

Tip: You can enjoy them right now, put them in a cookie jar or put them in a box. You could even place them in a small napkin to take them on a picnic!

Imaginary

Worlds

Howl's Moving Castle
CALCIFER'S BREAKFAST
FRIED EGGS, GRILLED BACON

LEVEL: *Easy* - SERVES: 4 - PREPARATION TIME: *10 min* - COOKING TIME: *10 min*

The old woman who has just joined the household tires you and intrigues you at the same time: she knows nothing about magic or Mr. Hauru's habits, whom she doesn't know either, and now she wants to prepare breakfast! She'll still have to tame Calcifer! But... she manages to control the fire demon and cook bacon!

Ingredients

4 slices of smoked bacon each
0.2 inch (5 mm) thick
8 large fresh eggs
Pepper (optional)

ON THE SIDE
1 loaf of homemade bread (see Tips
on page 128) or store-bought bread
Black tea
Montgomery's Cheddar or
Emmental cheese
Chives or flat leaf parsley

1 • Maybe you think everyone would know how to cook bacon and eggs, but no! You will see that there is a knack to it... There are two things to know about this recipe: it is best to braise the meat and use a cast iron frying pan.

2 • Depending on the size of your pan, you may want to do this in two batches, i.e., 2 slices of bacon and 4 eggs at a time. Place the thick slices of bacon in the pan and place the pan over medium heat: the heat will gradually heat the metal and melt the fat of the bacon. This cooking process allows you to obtain a meat that is tender in the middle and crispy on the surface. Cook the bacon for 2 minutes before turning it over, then continue cooking.

3 • Once the bacon is well colored and cooked through, you should still have enough fat in the pan for the eggs. Break the eggs into the pan and fry them for 2 minutes. You can add pepper if you wish, but remember that they will be naturally salted by the bacon.

4 • Serve when the egg whites have solidified and before the yolk begins to harden. It should still be runny!

5 • Accompany these bacon & eggs with a nice slice of bread. You can also serve a thin slice of cheese, cheddar or emmental, which will go perfectly with your eggs. Finally, to start the day off right and give yourself a boost, accompany your meal with a good cup of black tea (a.Japanese kôcha or a hot Ceylon tea).

Tip: here, I reproduced the recipe as you can see it in the picture, by not adding anything else to the plates, but you can of course season your eggs, add parsley or chopped chives, beans with tomato... It's time to get creative and greedy!

SOSUKE'S SANDWICHES

BACON, SALAD, CHEDDAR AND JAPANESE MAYONNAISE

LEVEL: *Easy* - SERVES: *4 people* - PREPARATION TIME: *20 min* - COOKING TIME: *5 min*

It's hard to understand the tension and nervousness of grown-ups when you're 5 years old! Your mom takes good care of you, but this is not the first sandwich you have eaten in a car speeding down the coastline! It is, however, the first sandwich you share with a creature as cute as the one in thewater bucket on your lap!

Ingredients

FOR THE JAPANESE MAYONNAISE
2 egg yolks
1 tbsp. Dijon mustard
2 tbsp. of rice or cider vinegar
1 tbsp. lemon or yuzu juice
¾ cup plus 2 tablespoons (200 ml) of neutral vegetable oil
1 large pinch of nori powder
1 large pinch of salt
1 pinch of sugar

FOR THE SANDWICH
8 slices of bacon
8 slices of homemade bread (see Tips on page 128) or store-bought bread
8 large leaves of romaine lettuce
4 slices of young cheddar cheese
4 green shiso leaves

1 • Prepare the Japanese mayonnaise to garnish the sandwiches: in a bowl, pour the egg yolks and mustard. Whisk lightly, then whisk in the vinegar and lemon juice. Add a thin layer of vegetable oil. Continue whisking until the mayonnaise begins to set then sprinkle in the nori powder, salt and sugar. Your mayonnaise should be light and creamy. Clingfilm and keep in the refrigerator while you prepare the next part.

2 • Next prepare the bacon: place it in a cold pan over medium heat. Let the fat melt and fry the bacon slices for 5 minutes, turning them over regularly. Place them on a paper towel Now your ingredients are ready, let's put the sandwiches together.

3 • For each sandwich, follow this order for the ingredients, from bottom to top: coat 2 slices of bread with Japanese mayonnaise, then place 1 sheet of romaine lettuce, 1 slice of cheddar cheese, then 2 slices of grilled bacon, 1 green shiso leaf, 1 romaine lettuce leaf and finish with 1 slice coated with mayonnaise.

All that's left to do is enjoy your sandwich!

Tip: for even more deliciousness, coat the outside of the bread slices with butter, then brown the sandwiches for 30 seconds under the grill at 428°F (220°C / Gas Mark 7-8).

Ponyo

SHIO RAMEN

CHINTAN BROTH, SHIO TARE, CHASHU PORK AND AJITSUKE TAMAGO

LEVEL: *Easy* - SERVES: *4* - PREPARATION TIME: *30 min* - COOKING TIME: *15 min*

You were convinced that you would never see your strange friend again after your misadventure under the dam. You were inconsolable yet now here she is again, changed, as if transformed, but you have no doubt, it's Ponyo! To warm up your body and heart, your mother concocts her classic ramen...

Ingredients

FOR THE CHINTAN BROTH
2 cups (500 ml) kombu and katsuobushi broth (see Tips page 114)
2 cups (500 ml) chicken stock (see Tips page 117)

FOR THE SHIO TARE
1⅓ cups (400 ml) chicken stock (see Tips page 117)
5 tablespoons (90 g) fine salt
2½ tablespoons (35 g) caster sugar
scant ½ cup (100 ml) cooking sake
½ cup (120 ml) of mirin

FOR THE AJITSUKE TAMAGO (PICKLED EGGS)
eggs + 1¼ cups (300 ml) of salted soy sauce
Or: 2 hard-boiled eggs

ON THE SIDE
spring onion
4 large slices of chashu pork or ham with herbs
4 portions of instant noodles
4 tsp. toasted sesame oil

1 • First prepare the pickled eggs: you can of course use hard-boiled eggs, but for authentic ramen eggs, bring a large volume of water to a boil, put the eggs in it for 5 min and 55 sec. Meanwhile, prepare a large volume of very cold or ice water. When the eggs have finished cooking, remove them from the boiling water and immediately place them in the cold water to stop the cooking process. Place the eggs in a bowl. Cover them with soy sauce and let them sit for the rest of the preparation. You can make more eggs at the same time, marinating them in the same way for up to 24 hours.

2 • Now move onto the shio tare: pour all the ingredients into a saucepan and heat over medium heat. Bring to a gentle boil, then cover and set aside over a low heat.

3 • Next prepare the chintan broth: in a large saucepan, pour the chicken stock and the kombu and katsuobushi broth. Bring to a gentle boil, then cover and set aside over a low heat.

4 • Finally, prepare the toppings: chop the green onion. Slice the pork in half. Quickly slice the eggs in half so that the runny yolk remains within the cooked and marinated white.

5 • Divide the noodles among 4 ramen bowls. Add 2 ladles of chintan broth and 1 small ladle of shio tare. Cover and let the noodles cook for 2 to 3 minutes. Then add 1 tsp. of sesame oil. Place half a marinated soft-boiled egg on the surface of the broth. Add 2 half slices of ham or chashu pork, then finish by scattering the onion green. Enjoy these bowls of ramen piping hot!

Note: in the movie, Sosuke's mother Lisa gives an instant ramen to the children. I prefer to put you on the path of homemade ramen, an exciting and endless art, by offering you a recipe that respects some basic principles: a strong broth, an aromatic oil, a tasty tare (the seasoning that gives the ramen its specificity) and carefully prepared toppings.

Tales from Earthsea
TENAR'S INVIGORATING SOUP
VEGETABLE SOUP WITH PROVENCAL HERBS

LEVEL: *Easy* - SERVES: *4* - PREPARATION TIME: *15 min* - COOKING TIME: *1h*

There are few doors that remain closed to the Hawk Mage: his help and wisdom are always welcome. That's why you're glad to have him back and don't hesitate for a second to welcome him and his wounded companion into your home. A vegetable soup is simmering on the stove, an opportunity to share a bowl with your old friend!

Ingredients

2 onions
2 carrots
1 stalk of celery
3 cloves of garlic
6 small new turnips
⅔ cup (100 g) canned organic white beans
¼ cup (50 g) pitted green olives

6 button mushrooms
4⅓ cups (500 g) organic tomato coulis (datterini)
6⅓ cups (1.5 litres) vegetable or poultry stock (see Tips page 117)
1 bouquet garni
1 tbsp. dried rosemary
Olive oil
Salt, pepper

1 • Prepare the vegetables and the aromatic garnish: peel and cut the onions and the carrots in the mirepoix style. Chop the celery stalk. Peel and coarsely chop the garlic cloves. Rinse, dry and cut the turnips into quarters. Drain and rinse the white beans and olives. Remove the stems from the mushrooms and gently clean them with a damp paper towel. Set all the ingredients aside.

2 • The vegetables are ready, now for the cooking: in a casserole dish, pour a good drizzle of olive oil and heat over medium heat. Once the oil is hot, sweat the onions, carrots and celery and let simmer, covered, for 20 minutes, stirring regularly.

3 • Stir in the garlic, turnips and white beans. Season with salt and sauté for 2 minutes, also stirring in the aromatic garnish. Pour in the tomato coulis and broth. Check the seasoning and adjust accordingly. Mix well and add the bouquet garni and rosemary. Bring to a simmer, cover and let simmer on a low heat for an additional 30 minutes.

4 • Finally, add the mushrooms and olives and continue to let simmer, covered, for 10 minutes. Best served hot!

Tip: You can add noodles, pasta or potatoes to give your soup more substance.

Kiki's Delivery Service
MADAME'S PIE
HERRING AND PUMPKIN PIE

LEVEL: *Medium* - SERVES: *4* - PREPARATION TIME: *30 min* - COOKING TIME: *35 min*

It's not easy being a rookie witch starting a home delivery business! Luckily, you sometimes work for caring and attentive customers! One of them needs you to help her bake her herring pie before delivering it: her oven just broke down and she wanted to deliver this pie to her granddaughter for her birthday... The pie looks delicious, why don't you ask for the recipe?

Ingredients

14 ounces (400 g) of herring fillet or cod back, prepared by your fishmonger
4⅓ cups (500 g) prepared pumpkin or kabucha
2 shortcrust pastry sheets of 7 ounces (200 g) each
Butter for the mold
Flour for working the dough
Olive oil
Salt, pepper

FOR THE BÉCHAMEL SAUCE
A few sprigs of tarragon or flat parsley
1 tbsp. (15 g) vegetable oil or soft butter
2½ tbsp. (15 g) flour
1 large pinch of salt
1 tbsp + 2 tsp (25 cl) of milk or dashi
1 pinch of grated nutmeg

FOR COOKING AND DRESSING
1 egg yolk + 1 tbsp. milk
Olive oil
Pepper, sansho pepper

Equipment

Pressure cooker or bamboo steamer basket
Potato masher (optional)
Rolling pin

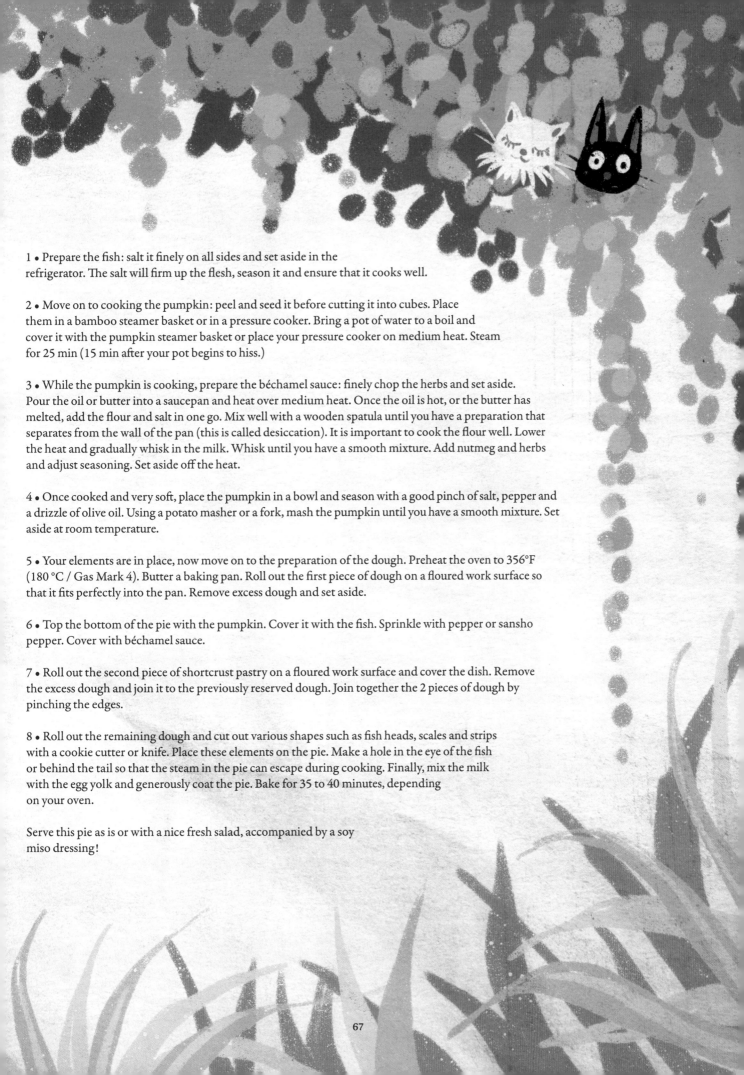

1 • Prepare the fish: salt it finely on all sides and set aside in the
refrigerator. The salt will firm up the flesh, season it and ensure that it cooks well.

2 • Move on to cooking the pumpkin: peel and seed it before cutting it into cubes. Place
them in a bamboo steamer basket or in a pressure cooker. Bring a pot of water to a boil and
cover it with the pumpkin steamer basket or place your pressure cooker on medium heat. Steam
for 25 min (15 min after your pot begins to hiss.)

3 • While the pumpkin is cooking, prepare the béchamel sauce: finely chop the herbs and set aside.
Pour the oil or butter into a saucepan and heat over medium heat. Once the oil is hot, or the butter has
melted, add the flour and salt in one go. Mix well with a wooden spatula until you have a preparation that
separates from the wall of the pan (this is called desiccation). It is important to cook the flour well. Lower
the heat and gradually whisk in the milk. Whisk until you have a smooth mixture. Add nutmeg and herbs
and adjust seasoning. Set aside off the heat.

4 • Once cooked and very soft, place the pumpkin in a bowl and season with a good pinch of salt, pepper and
a drizzle of olive oil. Using a potato masher or a fork, mash the pumpkin until you have a smooth mixture. Set
aside at room temperature.

5 • Your elements are in place, now move on to the preparation of the dough. Preheat the oven to 356°F
(180 °C / Gas Mark 4). Butter a baking pan. Roll out the first piece of dough on a floured work surface so
that it fits perfectly into the pan. Remove excess dough and set aside.

6 • Top the bottom of the pie with the pumpkin. Cover it with the fish. Sprinkle with pepper or sansho
pepper. Cover with béchamel sauce.

7 • Roll out the second piece of shortcrust pastry on a floured work surface and cover the dish. Remove
the excess dough and join it to the previously reserved dough. Join together the 2 pieces of dough by
pinching the edges.

8 • Roll out the remaining dough and cut out various shapes such as fish heads, scales and strips
with a cookie cutter or knife. Place these elements on the pie. Make a hole in the eye of the fish
or behind the tail so that the steam in the pie can escape during cooking. Finally, mix the milk
with the egg yolk and generously coat the pie. Bake for 35 to 40 minutes, depending
on your oven.

Serve this pie as is or with a nice fresh salad, accompanied by a soy
miso dressing!

A CHOCOLATE CAKEFOR KIKI

DOUBLE CHOCOLATE CAKE

LEVEL: *Medium* - SERVES: 4 - PREPARATION TIME: 45 min - COOKING TIME: 30 min - REST TIME: 1h 15

Oh what a pleasure to be offered a beautiful chocolate cake just for yourself! This old lady is really a sweet and generous person. We'll have to manage to bring this cake back on a broom without dropping it!

Ingredients

7 ounces (200 g) chocolate frosting (see Tips page 130)

FOR THE SPONGE CAKE
1 tbsp. + 2 tsp. (25 g) butter
4 whole eggs
1 pinch of salt
½ cup (120 g) powdered sugar
⅓ cups (100 g) flour
2 tbsp. (25 g) bitter cocoa powder
Scant ¼ cup (50 ml) umeshu (Japanese plum liqueur) (optional)

FOR THE CHOCOLATE WHIPPED CREAM
1½ cups (350 ml) heavy (double) cream (minimum 30% fat)
2 tbsp. (25 g) powdered sugar
2 tbsp. (25 g) bitter cocoa powder

FOR THE WHITE CHOCOLATE DECORATIONS
5¼ ounces (150 g) of white chocolate
Green food coloring,
Red food coloring

Equipment

Cake tin
Whisk or electric mixer
Piping bags
Silicone tray

1 • Place a round-bottomed mixing bowl
in the refrigerator. Butter the cake tin and prepare
the homemade frosting, or keep it at room temperature.

2 • Preheat the oven to 356°F (180 °C / Gas Mark 4). Let's prepare the chocolate
sponge cake. In a saucepan, melt the butter over low heat and set aside. Separate the yolks
and egg whites into 2 large bowls. Sprinkle the whites with salt. Using a mixer or whisk, beat
the egg whites until stiff and set aside. Pour the sugar into the bowl containing the yolks. Whisk
vigorously until the mixture is frothy and almost white. Set aside for a few minutes. Thoroughly
mix together the flour and cocoa powder. Sift and fold into the yolk-sugar mixture. Once your base
is chocolatey, gradually add the stiffly beaten egg whites until you obtain a smooth mixture. Finally,
add the melted butter.

3 • Pour the mixture into the cake tin and bake for 30 minutes. Turn out and place the cake on a rack
to let it rest at room temperature.

4 • For the chocolate whipped cream, nothing complicated: pour the heavy cream into the bottom of the
bowl previously removed from the refrigerator and mix it with the powdered sugar and cocoa powder. Then,
using the whisk, whip the mixture into a firm cream. Put it in a piping bag fitted with a round tip and set
aside in the refrigerator.

5 • Using a knife, slowly cut the sponge cake in half in thickness. Put one half of the cake on a rack, placed on
top of a tray, a drip pan, or any other large container. You can choose to soak the cake in a scant ¼ cup (50 ml) of
umeshu, a Japanese plum liqueur. Or you can simply top it generously with chocolate whipped cream and cover
the cream with the remaining half of the sponge cake.

6 • Cover the cake with the chocolate frosting, making sure to coat the entire cake evenly. Use a spatula to
remove excess frosting. Set aside for a few moments.

7 • Move on to creating the chocolate decorations: in a double boiler (bain-marie), melt the white chocolate.
You can temper it (controlling temperature and the cooling process) to make it firm and shiny once the
melted chocolate hardens. Otherwise, once melted, separate it into 2 bowls: ⅔ in one bowl, ⅓ in the other.
Cover a baking sheet with a silicone tray and pour ⅔ of the white chocolate. Using a spatula, spread it out
to 0.2 inches (5 mm) thickness. Set aside for a few moments in the refrigerator while the chocolate sets.
Separate the remaining white chocolate into 2 small bowls: add green coloring to the first and red coloring
to the second. Pour the chocolates on a small surface covered with a silicone sheet and place them
in the refrigerator for a few minutes.

8 • Once the chocolate is set, remove it from the refrigerator and cut out the shapes you need.
Cut out the letters using a stencil (see page 131), as well as the tree and the red bow.
Place them on the surface of the cake as the frosting is starting to set.

Your all-chocolate cake is ready to be eaten!

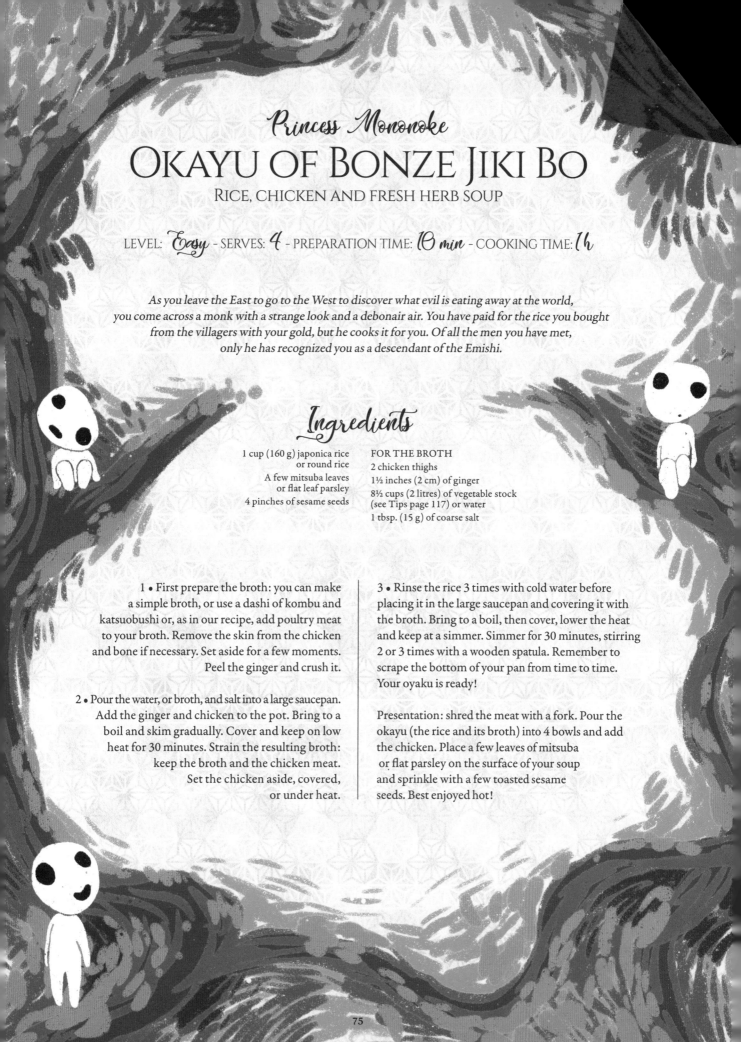

OKAYU OF BONZE JIKI BO

RICE, CHICKEN AND FRESH HERB SOUP

LEVEL: *Easy* - SERVES: *4* - PREPARATION TIME: *10 min* - COOKING TIME: *1 h*

As you leave the East to go to the West to discover what evil is eating away at the world, you come across a monk with a strange look and a debonair air. You have paid for the rice you bought from the villagers with your gold, but he cooks it for you. Of all the men you have met, only he has recognized you as a descendant of the Emishi.

Ingredients

1 cup (160 g) japonica rice
or round rice
A few mitsuba leaves
or flat leaf parsley
4 pinches of sesame seeds

FOR THE BROTH
2 chicken thighs
1½ inches (2 cm) of ginger
8½ cups (2 litres) of vegetable stock
(see Tips page 117) or water
1 tbsp. (15 g) of coarse salt

1 • First prepare the broth: you can make a simple broth, or use a dashi of kombu and katsuobushi or, as in our recipe, add poultry meat to your broth. Remove the skin from the chicken and bone if necessary. Set aside for a few moments. Peel the ginger and crush it.

2 • Pour the water, or broth, and salt into a large saucepan. Add the ginger and chicken to the pot. Bring to a boil and skim gradually. Cover and keep on low heat for 30 minutes. Strain the resulting broth: keep the broth and the chicken meat. Set the chicken aside, covered, or under heat.

3 • Rinse the rice 3 times with cold water before placing it in the large saucepan and covering it with the broth. Bring to a boil, then cover, lower the heat and keep at a simmer. Simmer for 30 minutes, stirring 2 or 3 times with a wooden spatula. Remember to scrape the bottom of your pan from time to time. Your oyaku is ready!

Presentation: shred the meat with a fork. Pour the okayu (the rice and its broth) into 4 bowls and add the chicken. Place a few leaves of mitsuba or flat parsley on the surface of your soup and sprinkle with a few toasted sesame seeds. Best enjoyed hot!

Castle in the Sky

AIRCRAFT CURRY
JAPANESE-STYLE BEEF CURRY WITH VEGETABLES

LEVEL: *Easy* - SERVES: *4* - PREPARATION TIME: *20 min* - COOKING TIME: *4 h 30*

There are many tasks that must be performed on Dora's gang's aircraft in order for it to fly! Many of them are thankless and dangerous, which is probably why all the crew members try to escape them by going to the kitchen to help Sheeta while she prepares a fabulous curry!

Ingredients

FOR THE BEEF STEW
1 pound 7 ounces (800 g) of beef (cheek, top rump, or chuck steak)
¼ ounces (150 g) smoked bacon
4 large carrots
4 shallots
2 cloves of garlic
2 onions
8½ cups (2 litres) vegetable broth or katsuobushi and kombu dashi (see Tips on page 114)
scant ½ cup (100 ml) of salted soy sauce
scant ¼ cup (50 ml) of sake
2 tbsp. liquid honey
4 dried shiitakes
1 bouquet garni
6 Charlotte potatoes
Sunflower oil
Salt

FOR THE CURRY PASTE
1½ tbsp. (20 g) butter or neutral vegetable oil
2½ tbsp. (20 g) flour
1 ½ tbsp. garam masala mix
1 tsp. ground curry powder
¾ inch (1 cm) fresh ginger
1 clove of garlic
2 tbsp. of salted soy sauce
1 tsp. of mirin or rice or cider vinegar
1 tsp. of concentrate or coulis of tomatoes
1 tsp. applesauce or ½ apple, coarsely grated
1 tsp. chili paste (optional)

FOR DRESSING
½ square of dark dessert chocolate

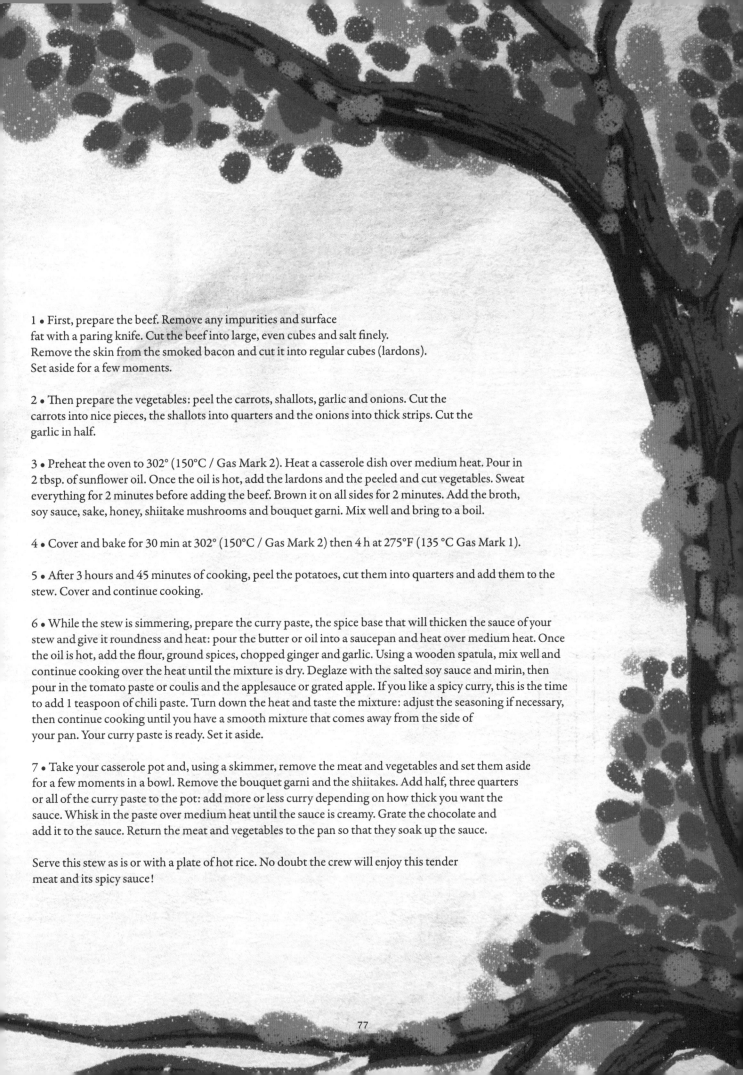

1 • First, prepare the beef. Remove any impurities and surface
fat with a paring knife. Cut the beef into large, even cubes and salt finely.
Remove the skin from the smoked bacon and cut it into regular cubes (lardons).
Set aside for a few moments.

2 • Then prepare the vegetables: peel the carrots, shallots, garlic and onions. Cut the
carrots into nice pieces, the shallots into quarters and the onions into thick strips. Cut the
garlic in half.

3 • Preheat the oven to 302° (150°C / Gas Mark 2). Heat a casserole dish over medium heat. Pour in
2 tbsp. of sunflower oil. Once the oil is hot, add the lardons and the peeled and cut vegetables. Sweat
everything for 2 minutes before adding the beef. Brown it on all sides for 2 minutes. Add the broth,
soy sauce, sake, honey, shiitake mushrooms and bouquet garni. Mix well and bring to a boil.

4 • Cover and bake for 30 min at 302° (150°C / Gas Mark 2) then 4 h at 275°F (135 °C Gas Mark 1).

5 • After 3 hours and 45 minutes of cooking, peel the potatoes, cut them into quarters and add them to the
stew. Cover and continue cooking.

6 • While the stew is simmering, prepare the curry paste, the spice base that will thicken the sauce of your
stew and give it roundness and heat: pour the butter or oil into a saucepan and heat over medium heat. Once
the oil is hot, add the flour, ground spices, chopped ginger and garlic. Using a wooden spatula, mix well and
continue cooking over the heat until the mixture is dry. Deglaze with the salted soy sauce and mirin, then
pour in the tomato paste or coulis and the applesauce or grated apple. If you like a spicy curry, this is the time
to add 1 teaspoon of chili paste. Turn down the heat and taste the mixture: adjust the seasoning if necessary,
then continue cooking until you have a smooth mixture that comes away from the side of
your pan. Your curry paste is ready. Set it aside.

7 • Take your casserole pot and, using a skimmer, remove the meat and vegetables and set them aside
for a few moments in a bowl. Remove the bouquet garni and the shiitakes. Add half, three quarters
or all of the curry paste to the pot: add more or less curry depending on how thick you want the
sauce. Whisk in the paste over medium heat until the sauce is creamy. Grate the chocolate and
add it to the sauce. Return the meat and vegetables to the pan so that they soak up the sauce.

Serve this stew as is or with a plate of hot rice. No doubt the crew will enjoy this tender
meat and its spicy sauce!

The Cat Returns

COOKIES FOR AN ORPHAN

BUTTER AND LEMON SHORTBREAD

LEVEL: *Easy* - SERVES: *4* - PREPARATION TIME: *15 min* - REST TIME: *10 min* - COOKING TIME: *10 min*

You saved a cat's life today. You had to tell her about it so that your mother remembered the time when, as a child, you told her that you talked to cats; and that's when your encounter with this little white, malnourished cat came back to you... Attracted by this little animal, you offered her some butter cookies. What did they taste like?

Ingredients

1½ cups (180 g) flour + a little
to work with
1 tbsp. (60 g) sugar
1 sachet vanilla sugar
⅔ cup (60 g) almond powder

1 pinch of salt
¾ cup (140 g) soft butter
1 egg
1 organic lemon

Equipment

Fish-shaped cookie cutters
Greaseproof paper
Clingfilm

1 • First prepare the cookie dough: sift all the dry ingredients into a mixing bowl. Mix well. Melt the butter and add to the dry ingredients. Add the egg and stir in until you have a smooth mixture. Zest the lemon and add the zest to the mixture.

2 • Remove the dough from the bowl and film it before placing it in the refrigerator for 45 minutes, until the butter sets.

3 • Preheat oven to 338°F (170°C / Gas Mark 3 approx.).

4 • Flour your work surface and roll out your dough with a rolling pin to a thickness of .40 inches (1 cm). Using the cookie cutter, cut out the shapes and place the fish on a baking sheet covered with greaseproof paper.

5 • Bake for 10 minutes then place the cookies on a rack.

Enjoy them once they have cooled down.

The Secret World of Arrietty
POD'S CREAMY TOAST

FARMHOUSE TARTINE WITH CHEESE, WILD MUSHROOMS, AND GARLIC BUTTER

LEVEL: *Easy* - SERVES: *4 persons* - PREPARATION TIME: *15 min* - COOKING TIME: *30 min*

You feel terribly guilty that your encounter with this young boy is forcing you to move out and give up the house your parents cared so much about. You don't feel judgment but love in your father's eyes as he offers you a slice of bread with a piece of melted cheese on it...

Ingredients

1 truckle (wheel) of farmhouse Mont-d'Or cheese

4 thick slices of homemade bread or brioche (see Tips on pages 127 and 128) or store-bought bread

¼ cup plus 3 tbsp. (100 g) semi-salted butter, at room temperature

6 wild garlic leaves

3½ ounces (100 g) of chanterelle mushrooms

3½ ounces (100 g) of oyster mushrooms

3½ ounces (100 g) brown mushrooms or shiitakes

1 bunch of flat parsley

Peanut oil

Fleur de sel, ground pepper

Equipment

Flexible spatula
Aluminum foil

1 • Preheat oven to 375°F (190°C / Gas Mark 5). Prepare the wild garlic butter: chop the wild garlic finely and place it in a round-bottomed mixing bowel. Add the soft butter and mix in with a flexible spatula. Set aside.

2 • Prepare the mushrooms: clean them delicately with a damp paper towel, then cut the chanterelles and oyster mushrooms in half and the brown mushrooms in quarters. Chop the flat parsley.

3 • Wrap the base of your cheese truckle in a sheet of aluminum foil, place it on a baking tray and bake for 20 minutes.

4 • In the meantime, move on to cooking the mushrooms: pour a drizzle of oil into a frying pan and heat it over high heat. Once the oil is hot, add the brown mushrooms and oyster mushrooms and sauté for 4 to 5 minutes. Then add the chanterelles and flat-leaf parsley. Continue

cooking for 1½ minutes before removing the mushrooms to a surface covered with a paper towel. Place them on a plate and sprinkle them finely with fleur de sel and ground pepper. Set aside.

5 • A few moments before removing the cheese from the oven, brush the bread slices with wild garlic butter and put them in the oven for 2 minutes.

Presentation: for each guest, place a large spoonful of mushrooms on a slice of golden bread buttered with wild garlic. Pour a generous amount of melted cheese over the mushrooms and enjoy!

Note: in the film, the meal is more frugal and the toast much simpler. We see a nice slice of bread covered with melted cheese. I wanted to offer you an alternative, with ingredients that the thieves could have found in the woods (they of course knew how to melt cheese, at least!).

The Secret World of Arrietty
A Quiet Meal with Aunt Sadako

Marinated tournedos, steamed broccoli, noodles, and sesame oil

LEVEL: *Easy* - SERVES: *4* - PREPARATION TIME: *20 min* - COOKING TIME: *12 + 10 min* - REST TIME: *30 min to 12 h*

Aunt Sadako really is a sweet and caring person. When you share a meal, she never fails to tell you about your family history. Today, she mentioned the existence of little people, which attracted your attention...

Ingredients

4 tournedos
1 broccoli
1 dash of sesame oil
1 tbsp. sesame seeds
Sunflower oil
Fleur de sel, pepper

FOR THE BEEF MARINADE
2 shallots
¾ inch (1 cm) ginger
1 tsp. miso
2½ tbsp. (30 g) sugar or
1 tbsp. honey
scant 1 cup (200 ml) soy sauce
3½ tbsp. (50 ml) mirin
3½ tbsp. (50 ml) of olive oil

ON THE SIDE
8½ ounces (240 g) cooked noodles
⅔ cup (120 g) cooked rice

Equipment

Steamer basket
Flexible spatula

1 • First, marinate the meat: salt it finely and set it aside for a while. Peel and chop the shallots and ginger. Pour the miso paste and the sugar into a mixing bowl. Work the mixture with a flexible spatula to incorporate the ingredients. Add the soy sauce, mirin, olive oil, ginger and shallots. Mix well and dip the meat in it. Cover and place in the refrigerator for at least 30 minutes (maximum 12 hours).

2 • Before cooking the meat, move on to cooking the broccoli: Trim the tops of the broccoli. Rinse them with fresh water. Then place them in a steamer basket. Bring a large volume of water to a boil and place the basket on top. Steam the broccoli for 12 minutes. Set them aside for a few moments. Pour the sesame oil and seeds into a bowl. Place the broccoli on top and coat well with the mixture. Set it aside.

3 • Move on to cooking the meat: remove the meat from its marinade and place it on a surface covered with paper towels. Place the marinade over medium heat to make a teriyaki sauce: stir regularly and reduce over low heat. Cook in a medium saucepan for 5 to 10 minutes until syrupy. Drizzle sunflower oil into a skillet (ideally cast iron) and heat over high heat. Once the pan and oil are hot, place the tournedos on top. Cook them two by two. Mark each side well for at least 30 seconds, then lower the heat to medium and continue cooking according to your preference. Once cooked, place the meat on a resting rack or on your cutting board and allow it to rest for several minutes before cutting and tasting it: resting time should be half the time taken to cook.

Presentation: Cut each tournedos into thick bites and serve with sesame broccoli and teriyaki sauce. Accompany this dish with noodles and a bowl of white rice. Enjoy your meal!

Note: to change up this dish, don't hesitate to replace broccoli with broccolinis!

The Secret World of Arriëtty

THE BORROWERS' CREAMY STEW

BROTH AND VEGETABLES, LIGHT BÉCHAMEL SAUCE

LEVEL: *Easy* - SERVES: *4* - PREPARATION TIME: *15 min* - COOKING TIME: *45 min*

It seems someone has left you a sugar cube on the windowsill. You think it's the piece you lost yesterday, but your mother seems to think it's more likely a trick the big people are playing to capture you... Everything in your daily life will probably have to change. Before you consider what the future has in store, why not eat some of that creamy stew while it's still hot?

Ingredients

2 cloves of garlic
1½ inches (2 cm) of fresh ginger
4 large carrots
4 potatoes
½ broccoli
8½ cups (2 litres) vegetable stock
(see Tips on page 117)
1 tbsp. cooking sake
1 tbsp. soy sauce
A few leaves of flat parsley

FOR THE BÉCHAMEL SAUCE
1½ tbsp. (20 g) vegetable oil
2½ tbsp. (20 g) flour
1 large pinch of salt
1 large pinch of pepper
1 cup (250 ml) of milk

1 • Prepare the vegetables first. Crush the garlic. Crush the ginger with the palm of your hand or under the blade of a paring knife. Peel the carrots and potatoes. Cut them into quarters. Cut the tops off the broccoli. Now it's time to get cooking!

2 • In a large casserole dish, combine the broth and all the vegetables and bring to a boil. Pour in the sake and soy sauce. Mix well and cover. Lower the heat to medium and continue cooking for 45 minutes.

3 • Meanwhile, make the béchamel sauce: pour the vegetable oil into a saucepan and heat it over medium heat. Once the oil is hot, add the flour and salt. Mix well and continue to cook the paste for 1½ minutes, while stirring to prevent it from sticking. Once the paste is well-cooked, remove the pan

from the heat and whisk in the milk until you have a béchamel sauce. Season with pepper and salt. Set aside in the pan, off the heat.

4 • Once the vegetables are cooked through and tender, separate and remove the vegetables from the broth by straining it. Remove the ginger. Return the pan of béchamel to medium heat and whisk in the broth. Add broth as desired, but remember that the more broth you add, the less creamy it will be.

Presentation: pour the creamy broth into 4 bowls and add the melting vegetables in the middle. Finally, garnish with flat-leaf parsley and enjoy hot!

Ô-BABA'S SOUP
SALICORNIA AND WHITE BEAN SOUP

LEVEL: *Easy* - SERVES: *4* - PREPARATION TIME: *15 min* - COOKING TIME: *40 min*

You are very happy to find your old tutor, the wise Yupa. Because he is important and respected, you accompany him to the bedside of King Jill and the great old woman Ô-Baba, who is preparing a soup that smells of the sea...

Ingredients

2 shallots
1¼ cup (250 g) canned white beans
5¼ ounces (150 g) of fresh salicornia
¾ inch (1 cm) of fresh ginger
2 cloves of garlic

4¼ cups (1 litre) of kombu and katsuobushi dashi or vegetable broth (see Tips on page 117)
A few pinches of shichimi togarashi or ground Espelette pepper
Olive oil
Fleur de sel

Equipment

Hand blender

1 • Prepare the vegetables. Peel and chop the shallots. Drain and rinse the beans. Rinse the salicornia and chop them coarsely. Peel the ginger and garlic and chop them finely.

2 • In a saucepan, bring the broth to a simmer.

3 • In a casserole dish, pour a dash of olive oil and heat over medium heat. Sweat the shallots for 2 minutes. Then add the salicornia, garlic and ginger and sauté for 5 minutes before adding the beans. Season to taste. Continue cooking for 2 minutes before adding the broth (about 3 cups or 700 ml). Cover and simmer for 10 minutes, until the vegetables absorb the broth and are tender. Do not hesitate to continue to cook for a few minutes if the vegetables are not soft enough.

4 • Using a hand blender, blend the mixture to a smooth cream. Add the remaining broth according to your preferred consistency, from creamy to liquid.

Serve this soup hot and sprinkle it with fleur de sel and shichimi togarashi (or ground Espelette pepper) to spice up the taste. Enjoy your meal!

BATHHOUSE NIKUMAN

STEAMED BREAD, ANKO

LEVEL: *Easy* - SERVES: *4* - PREPARATION TIME: *20 min* - REST TIME: *1h 30* - COOKING TIME: *10 min per nikuman*

Since you joined Yubaba's service, you don't have a minute to yourself: at the oven and the mill managing the water of the baths with old Kamaji or polishing the floors with Lin. Sometimes, when night falls, you could almost fall asleep without eating. However, a bite of these delicious nikuman would do you a world of good!

Ingredients

2½ cups (300 g) pureed azuki beans
or homemade anko paste
(see Tips on page 129)

FOR THE NIKUMAN DOUGH
2⅓ cups (280 g) wheat flour + a little
for the work surface
1 tbsp. (18 g) sugar
1 pinch salt
1 level teaspoon of baking powder
1 level teaspoon of yeast
½ cup (120 ml) of warm water
(86°F / 30°C max)

Equipment

Steamer basket
Greaseproof paper

1 • First prepare the nikuman dough: in a mixing bowl, pour all the dry ingredients. Mix them and dig a well in the center. Pour the water inside. Lightly flour your hands and knead with your fingertips until smooth. Flour the work surface and place the dough on top. Knead until you have a smooth ball. Place the dough in another bowl. Cover with a cloth and let the dough rise for 1 hour at room temperature.

2 • When the dough has rested, remove the cloth and press the dough with your fist to release the gas and allow it to lose its volume. Flour your work surface and place the dough ball on it. Shape it into a thick sausage and cut it into 10 even pieces. Roll each piece into a disk of about 4 inches (approx. 10 cm) in diameter.

3 • Take a disk in the palm of your hand and place in the centre 2 tbsp. of bean or homemade anko paste. Close the disc on itself by folding it into a palm. Repeat for each disc.

4 • Place a sheet of greaseproof paper in a steamer basket. Place the filled dough pieces on top and let them rest and rise for another 30 minutes.

5 • Once the nikuman are well risen, you can start cooking them. Under the steam basket, bring the water to a boil. Cook for 10 minutes. Keep at a boil on a medium heat, the steam does not need to be too strong. When the bread is done, remove it from the steamer basket and serve immediately.

Spirited Away

TEA-TIME WITH ZENIBA

SOUFFLÉ-STYLE JAPANESE CHEESECAKE

LEVEL: *Medium* - SERVES: *6* - PREPARATION TIME: *20 min* - REST TIME: *10 min* - COOKING TIME: *1h20min*

Although she looks like Yubaba, Zeniba, her twin sister, is made of different stuff: friendly and warm, she invites you to drink tea. Without giving you the solution to your problems, she finds a way to put you on the right track. You'd like a piece of cake, wouldn't you?

Ingredients

¾ cup (130 g) cream cheese spread
1 tbsp. (15 g) of soft butter
Scant ¼ cup (50 ml) of milk
3 eggs
4 tbsp. (50 g) sugar

2 tsp. (10 g) vanilla sugar
3 tbsp. + 2 tsp. (30 g) wheat flour
2 tbsp. (15 g) cornstarch
Liquid honey (for the finishing touch)

Equipment

Charlotte cake pan (mold)
Basting brush
Greaseproof paper

1 • Place the cream cheese and soft butter in a round-bottomed mixing bowl with the milk. Place the bowl in a double boiler (bain-marie), melt the butter and whisk it into the cheese and milk. Mix well until you obtain a smooth and creamy texture. Take it out of the double boiler and let it rest for 10 minutes at room temperature.

2 • Preheat the oven to 320°F (160°c / Gas Mark 3). Crack the eggs and separate the whites from the yolks. Keep the yolks to one side for the moment. Beat the whites until stiff. While whisking, mix in the sugars in 3 stages. Set aside.

3 • Fold the egg yolks into the cheese-milk-butter mixture. Then, gently fold in the meringue whites in three stages. Finally, mix in the flour and cornstarch. Sift and combine with the creamy mixture.

4 • Now it's time to bake: line the bottom of the Charlotte pan with greaseproof paper. Pour in the mixture. Tap the bottom of the pan against your work surface to prevent air bubbles.

5 • Line a large dish with a bed of paper towels or a cloth. Place the Charlotte pan on top. Bring water to a simmer and pour it into the dish so that the Charlotte pan is submerged about an inch (2–3 cm).

6 • Bake for 20 min then open the oven for 6 seconds so that the hot air can escape. Turn down the heat to 230°F (110°C / Gas Mark 1) and continue baking for 1 hour before removing your cake from the oven.

7 • Remove from the pan and place on a serving dish. Finally, to add the finish touch, gently brush its surface with honey.

Enjoy with a good tea and good company!

93

CURSED QUAILS

STUFFED LACQUERED QUAIL WITH CHILI AND THAI BASIL

LEVEL: *Medium* - SERVES: 4 - PREPARATION TIME: *30 min* - REST TIME: *1 h to 12 h* - COOKING TIME: *1 h*

You're just a kid, but you know your parents shouldn't be stuffing themselves without permission.
This park, so empty and mysterious, is home to a gargantuan buffet. Something is wrong…
but those stuffed quails do look appetizing!

Ingredients

4 quails emptied and prepared by your butcher
4¼ cups (1 litre) chicken broth (see Tips on page 117)
A few Thai basil leaves
Toasted sesame seeds
Salt

FOR THE MARINADE
2 cloves of garlic
¾ inch (1 cm) fresh ginger
1 tsp. paprika
⅔ cup (150 ml) soy sauce
scant ½ cup (100 ml) of rice vinegar
1 tbsp. sriracha sauce
4 tbsp. concentrated soy sauce
2 tbsp. oyster sauce
1 tsp. sesame oil
3 tbsp. rice syrup
1 tsp. five-spice

FOR THE STUFFING
2 tbsp. (30 g) canned bamboo shoots
8 shiitakes
10½ (300 g) ground pork or beef
2 tbsp. (30 g) fried shallots or onions
1 tsp. (5 g) of sugar
1½ tsp. (6 g) of salt
1 tsp. (5 g) black pepper
1 tsp. (5 g) five-spice
1 tbsp. of mirin
1 tbsp. soy sauce

1 • Start by preparing the marinade for the quails: salt them finely on all sides and also inside. Set them aside for a few moments.

2 • Peel and finely chop the garlic and ginger. Place them in a bowl and add all the ingredients for the marinade. Mix with a wooden spatula to obtain a smooth and fragrant mixture. Dip the quails in the marinade and cover with clingfilm. Place in the refrigerator for at least 1 hour and a maximum of 12 hours.

3 • Prepare the stuffing for the lacquered quails: Drain the bamboo shoots and chop them. Coarsely chop the shiitakes. Place the bamboo shoots, shiitakes and all the ingredients in a round-bottomed mixing bowl with the other ingredients for the stuffing. Mix all the ingredients with your hands to obtain a smooth texture for the filling. Clingfilm and set aside in the refrigerator.

4 • Preheat your oven to 356°F (180 °C / Gas Mark 4).

5 • Remove the quails from the marinade, setting the marinade aside. Using a piping bag or spoon, stuff the quails with the filling.

6 • Pour the marinade into a large ovenproof dish or broiler pan. Add the broth and quails. Bake for 1 hour, basting the birds regularly with the sauce.

Presentation: Serve the quails whole and hot. Sprinkle with toasted sesame seeds. Chop the Thai basil and place it on the quails. Serve with rice or a fresh salad!

Spirited Away
HAKU'S ONIGIRIS
JAPANESE RICE BALLS

LEVEL: *Medium* - SERVES: *4* - PREPARATION TIME: *30 min* - REST TIME: *10 min* - COOKING TIME: *15 min*

*Sometimes it takes nothing more than a simple rice dumpling from a friend
to remind you of the warmth of home...*

Ingredients

2 cups plus 2 tbsp. (400 g) koshihikari rice
(japonica or arborio)
scant 1 cup (200 ml) of rice vinegar
2 tbsp. (30 g) of caster sugar
½ tsp 2 g of salt

Equipment

Fan

1 • Rinse the rice several times (3 times minimum) until the rinsed water starts to look clearer. Pour the rice into a saucepan with 2 cups (500 ml) of water and bring to a boil. Let it cook for 12 minutes on a very low heat, then let the rice rest, covered and off the heat, for 10 minutes.

2 • Meanwhile, pour the vinegar, sugar and salt into a saucepan. Melt the sugar and salt over low heat but do not bring to a boil. Set aside.

3 • Collect the rice and place it in a large bowl. Pour ¾ of the vinegar mixture over it and mix well with a wooden spatula to avoid crushing the rice grains. Position a small table fan so that it cools the rice as you add the vinegar mixture. Your onigiri rice is ready.

4 • Moisten your hands with the remaining vinegar mixture so that the rice does not stick to your skin. Scoop out a portion of rice. Shape it into a ball between your palms. Repeat until all the ingredients are used up.

Enjoy these rice balls warm or at room temperature. So simple!

Note: if the onigiris offered to Chihiro by Haku seem simple, you should know that there are many recipes out there.

Tips

Fresh Produce

Garlic

Vegetable common to Japanese, Asian, Middle Eastern and Mediterranean gastronomy. It is used to flavor sautéed vegetables, to flavor oils and broths or rub on toasted bread. Its virtues are numerous and its taste is always powerful.

Japanese eggplant

Slightly different from our eggplant with its long and thin shape. You can fry it, preserve it, sauté it or marinate it with miso.

Carrot

It is used in many recipes in Japanese cuisine as in my favorite dish, the Japanese curry.

Mushrooms

Shimeji, enoki and shiitake mushrooms are widely used in Japanese cuisine. Shimeji and enoki mushrooms have a delicate taste and are commonly used in salads or broths.

Cucumber

One of the vegetables that can be found in raw salads or in tsukemono, which means vinegar, i.e., pickled.

Edamame

Young soybeans, very green; they are served cold as an appetizer or used in cooking similar to peas.

Fresh ginger

An essential ingredient in Japanese cuisine, it is used to flavor marinades, sauces, infusions and syrups.

Egg

Marinated in soy, in the shell, soft, perfect in onsen tamago, in an omelette, in mayonnaise, for cakes, custards, creams and even in cocktails, the applications of the egg are numerous. I always have some at home.

Onion

Whether they are yellow or new, onions are as present in Japanese cuisine as they are elsewhere. Because of their freshness, even sweetness when candied, onions have a wide aromatic palette.

Potato

Commonly used in Japan, in a sweet way or more classically salted in casseroles or fried in breadcrumbs.

Green Shiso

A plant whose leaves are used in traditional medicine as well as in cooking. Dark red or deep green in color, shiso is considered the Japanese basil.

Tofu

Tofu is a product of the curdling of soya milk. It is a white, soft, crumbly paste, sometimes firm, sometimes silky, with a neutral taste. Tofu is a food consumed daily in Asia.

Noodles

Noodles have been eaten in Japan since the 8th century AD. The first writings on this subject report that they originated in China. Over more than 1300 years, the Japanese have perfectly integrated them into their food and their cooking, honing their preparation and creating various recipes based on this key ingredient.

Nowadays, when we talk about Japanese noodles, we instantly think of ramen, those wheat noodles eaten in a broth full of flavors, but we can distinguish other noodle dishes, each region having its own recipes, its own know-how, etc.
Here are the most popular noodles in Japan:

Ramen

This term refers to both the dish and the noodles used to make it. Made from wheat flour and eggs, these noodles are thin and long. They are usually served in a hot broth, the ingredients and preparation of which vary according to the region.

Soba

Brown in color and a bit rough in texture, these buckwheat noodles are eaten daily in Japan. They are not traditionally eaten in broth but sautéed with vegetables, hot or cold, accompanied by tsuyu sauce.

Udon

These noodles are prepared with soft wheat and water. Thick, long and white, they are eaten hot, cold, in broth or sautéed. They are the easiest to make at home!

Some additional information on how noodles are prepared and eaten in Japan:

Generally, udon or ramen are rinsed before adding broth: rinsing them serves to remove the excess starch remaining on the surface of the noodles and making them stick together. The Japanese prefer them to be slippery so that they can be sucked up more easily (and with a lot of noise).

The Japanese attach great importance in cooking to the play of temperatures and textures between foods. This is why they alternate different noodles to play on the texture and different cooking (stir-fried or in broth) to create varieties of temperature. It is not uncommon to find cold noodle soups or noodles in salad.

Culinary

Here is a little glossary of Japanese words related to cooking. Please note that I don't speak Japanese, the idea is to explain clearly the meaning of these terms in a simple way.

A

AJITSUKE TAMAGO
Tamago means "egg". *Ajitsuke tamago* is an egg marinated in soy sauce, probably the most famous egg in Japanese cuisine.

ANKO PASTE
Creamy paste made from azuki or red beans: round, small and slightly sweet.

AONORI POWDER
The aonori is a dried and powdered green seaweed, used to season a dish or as a condiment.

C

CHASHU PORK
A preparation of pork belly marinated and cooked for a long time at low temperature. When cooled, it is sliced like a roast and served in ramen or as a topping for some dishes. Its name comes from the Chinese char siu pork.

CHINTAN BROTH
This term designates a clear broth (as opposed to the more opaque broths called *paitan*).

D

DASHI
Dashi is the typical Japanese broth, regularly made from kombu seaweed and dried and grated bonito.

E

EDAMAME
Young green soybeans. Eaten in a similar way to peas.

F

FURIKAKE POWDER
A mixture of salt, spices and seaweed used to season a dish.

G

GYOZA
Fried dumplings prepared in the Japanese style. They are inspired by the Chinese jiaozi.

Terms

K

KABUCHA
Japanese squash.

KASUTERA
This is the Japanese term for the Portuguese word *castella*, which designates a soft cake with an airy sponge, imported into Japan in the 16th century by Portuguese missionaries.

KATSUOBUSHI
Dried and grated bonito. It is used in broths but also as toppings to "give life" to preparations: the bonito reacts to heat, it seems that its pieces come to life and twirl over the dishes for a few moments.

KOMBU
Seaweed used in Japanese cooking. It can be found in Asian grocery stores in dried form.

KOROKKE
Japanese style potato croquettes.

M

MATCHA TEA
Japanese ground green tea. It has many uses. It is one of the most beautiful things that Japan has given to the rest of the world.

MIRIN
Sweetened and fermented rice wine, close to sake, it is used in Japanese cuisine very regularly.

MISO
Miso is one of the basic ingredients of Japanese cuisine. This fermented soybean paste is used for soups, broths or marinades.

MITSUBA
In Japan, this herb is used like parsley but has a stronger and more subtle aromatic power.

N

NIKUMAN
Stuffed and steamed breads, like baos.

O

ONIGIRI
Typical Japanese rice balls.

OYAKU
Japanese play on words for "parent" and "child" and refers to a dish of chicken and egg on a bed of rice.

P

PANKO BREADCRUMBS

The term panko refers to breadcrumbs or powder. In cooking, panko breadcrumbs are made from a crustless loaf of bread that is mixed and crumble roughly. Panko breadcrumbs are crazy crunchy and not as fine as our traditional breadcrumbs.

PONZU SAUCE

Typical Japanese sauce, made from soy sauce and Japanese citrus fruits.

R

RAMEN

One of the most famous Japanese dishes in the world. 5 elements distinguish the real bowl of ramen: a very fragrant broth, noodles, toppings (chashu pork, tamago, etc.), an aromatic oil and a "tare", the seasoning base.

S

SANSHO PEPPER

It is a pepper in name only, since it is in fact a berry, closer to a citrus fruit than to a pepper. "Sansho" means "mountain pepper." Typically Japanese, it has a fresh and lemony flavor.

SAKE

Sake, whether for cooking or drinking, is a traditional fermented rice alcohol of Japanese gastronomy. In Japanese, the word "sake" defines all types of alcohol without distinction. The Japanese use the term *nihonshu sake* to describe the aromatic drink that is unique to Japan.

SAKURA DENBU

A colorful fish preparation that displays the characteristic pink of Japanese cherry blossoms. It is a light, airy and delicious dish.

SENCHA TEA

The most cultivated and consumed green tea in Japan.

SHABU-SHABU

Japanese fondue, where food is cooked in a boiling broth. This dish gets its name from the sound of beef cooking in the broth.

SHICHIMI TOGARASHI

Japanese blend of seven ground spices. It contains dried red pepper, citrus peel, sesame seeds, poppy seeds, hemp seeds, aonori seeds and sansho.

SHIITAKE

Mushrooms native to Japan. Brilliant for giving body to broths, they are also delicious when stuffed or sautéed.

SHIMEJI MUSHROOMS

Mushroom native to Japan. Its base is rather long and its cap small and round. It is found in different sizes but often in small clusters.

SHIO TARE

"Tare" is the basis for seasoning a broth or ramen. "Shio" means salt. So "shio tare" is a preparation based on salt.

SHISO

Red or green, this aromatic plant originating from India or China is regularly consumed in Japan. It has a strong scent somewhere between basil and mint.

SOBA NOODLES

Buckwheat noodles.

T

TAMAGOYAKI

Literally "cooked eggs," it is a Japanese omelette rolled and folded on itself.

TEMPURA

Japanese frying technique, also brought to the Japanese archipelago by Portuguese missionaries. Many foods, such as vegetables and fish, can be prepared this way.

TSUYU SAUCE

Common sauce in Japan, made from a mixture of soy sauce, mirin and dashi.

U

UMEBOSHI

"Ume" means plum. Umeboshi is a pickled plum.

Y

YAKITORI

Traditionally, yakitoris are skewers of bite-sized grilled meat.

YŌKAN

Jellied fruit or red bean paste, a traditional Japanese pastry.

YUZU

Here is the most famous Japanese citrus fruit! Its zest and juice are powerful and subtle, the yuzu being a hybrid fruit born from the crossing of the lemon and tangerine.

Long-lasting

Azuki bean

Azuki beans are one of the main foods in Japan, similar to soybeans. They are used sweetened, boiled and in paste, with which dorayaki or nikuman are stuffed.

Furikake powder

Furikake powder is a concentrate of umami, the fifth flavor. It is used as a condiment on rice or noodles. Furikake is a mixture of salt, sugar, sesame and kelp. It is perfectly possible to make it yourself and to make your own version. My personal version: 1 tsp. of fleur de sel, 1 tsp. of nori powder, 1 tsp. of dried chili, 1 tsp. of sansho, 1 tsp. of toasted sesame. Add it all together and enjoy.

Gyoza dough

It can be bought fresh or frozen. Gyoza dough is made from a mixture of wheat flour, salt and water. It is very easy to make at home.

Katsuobushi

Sold in flakes or chips, katsuobushi is a Japanese preparation consisting of pieces of dried and fermented bonito. It is the second basic ingredient of dashi broth.

Kombu seaweed

Usually sold dried, kombu is an edible seaweed with a very iodized taste which is used as a basic ingredient in the making of dashi. Cold and fresh, it can be eaten as sashimi.

Matcha tea

Typical Japanese ground green tea. With its deep green color and powerful taste, this tea is used in everyday life, in ceremonies, but also in baking and cooking. It is my favorite tea.

Miso

A traditional food in Japanese cuisine, it is made from soybeans, rice or barley, salt, water and koji, a kind of fermentation culture. These ingredients are mixed together in varying proportions and fermented over a period of several weeks to several years. Miso is a great food in the kitchen, as it can be used to enhance a sauce, to marinate meat, to cook a simple broth or to season a dish. There are different varieties of miso including:

WHITE MISO
Rice miso, softer and with almost sweet notes.

RED MISO
Much more salty than white miso; its fermentation time is rather long.

GENMAI MISO
Whole grain rice miso, also very salty, although its flavor has a tangy side.

ingredients

Nori leaf

Initially red, nori seaweed turns green or black as it dries. Rich in proteins and taste, and iodized, nori is used in the preparation of certain sushi (temaki, maki, etc.), onigiri, and also in broths.

Panko breadcrumbs

Japanese breadcrumbs are quite special. Thicker and crisper than the fine breadcrumbs used in our kitchens, panko breadcrumbs get their texture from the fact that the bread they are made from is cooked by passing an electric current through the dough.

Koshihikari rice

For more information on rice, see page 116. Of the many varieties of rice grown in Japan, koshihikari rice is consistently recognized as the best in terms of taste. With its short, pearly, bright grains, it has a light and delicate flavor.

Sansho

Called pepper and used as such, sansho is in fact a berry of the prickly ash tree that grows on the mountainous massifs of Japan. This berry belongs to the Rutaceae family, like citrus fruits. This is the reason why this "pepper" brings particularly lemony and warm notes. You can find it in Asian or Japanese stores.

Shichimi togarashi

Traditional Japanese blend of 7 elements (sansho, dried red pepper, mandarin peel, sesame, poppy, hemp and nori or aonori). Created in the Edo era, it is used as a base for seasoning in many Japanese dishes.

Shiitake dried

Also known as the oak leaf, this edible mushroom originally comes from Asia. Very common in Chinese and Japanese cuisine, shiitake has interesting nutritional properties (rich in vitamins). Fresh, it can be pan-fried and cooked. Fresh or dried, it can easily be used to give power to a broth or an infusion.

Soba noodles

Buckwheat flour noodles, brown in color and widely used in the daily diet of the Japanese.

Wheat Somen

Durum wheat (hard wheat) noodles. Very fine, they are rich in proteins and minerals.

Yuzu kosho

Green or red pepper paste, salted and flavored with yuzu, a citrus fruit native to Japan. Used as a condiment, you can find it in Japanese or Asian grocery stores or on online.

Broths

Vegan Dashi broth

PREPARATION TIME: *5 min*

COOKING TIME: *15 min* – RESTING TIME: *30 min*

Ingredients

8½ cups (2 litres) spring water (or tap water)
¼ ounce (10 g) kombu algae
4 dried shiitakes
1 tbsp. vegan soy sauce

1 • Place the seaweed pieces and dried mushrooms
in a large saucepan, add the water and soy sauce.
Bring to a simmer and remove from heat.

2 • Leave to stand for 35 minutes, covered,
then strain the mixture. It's ready!

Dashi broth with dried bonito

(DASHI OF KATSUOBUSHI)

PREPARATION TIME: *5 min*

COOKING TIME: *15 min* – RESTING TIME: *30 min*

This broth is the aromatic base for
Japanese soups.

Ingredients

½ cups (2 litres) spring water (or tap water)
¼ ounce (10 g) kombu seaweed
1½ ounces (40 g) katsuobushi (grated dried bonito flakes)

1 • Place the seaweed pieces in a large saucepan,
add the water. Bring to a simmer and
add the bonito flakes. Bring to a simmer
and remove from heat.

2 • Let stand for 35 minutes, covered,
then strain the mixture. Your dashi is ready!

Beef broth

PREPARATION TIME: *10 min* – REST TIME: *1 h* – COOKING TIME: *4 h 30*

Ingredients

2¼ pounds (1 kg) inexpensive beef cuts
8½ cups (2 litres) of sparkling water
12¾ cups (3 litres) spring water
(or tap water)
1 large onion
2 carrots
1 leek
2 dried shiitakes

1 bouquet garni
1 clove
1 tbsp. + 2 tsp. (25 g) coarse salt
A few peppercorns
Grape seed oil
Salt

1 • 1 hour before cooking, prepare the meat: cut it into small cubes and keep the bones. Put the meat in a bowl and cover with sparkling water: it will collect some of the blood and impurities of the meat. Keep to one side in the refrigerator.

2 • Prepare the aromatic garnish: peel the onion and carrots. Cut them in mirepoix style. Rinse and dry the leek, remove its stale parts and cut them into slices, the green parts and the white. Set aside.

3 • In a cast iron casserole dish, pour 3 tbsp. of grape seed oil and heat over medium heat.
Place the vegetables in the casserole and brown them for 5 minutes, stirring regularly. Once the aromatic garnish begins to brown, remove it for a few moments.

4 • Place the casserole over high heat. Drain and dry the meat and salt it finely on all sides. Place the beef cubes and trimmings in the casserole. Brown everything well for 10 minutes. Stir with a wooden spoon and add the aromatic garnish. Add the mushrooms and the bouquet garni, as well as the clove, the coarse salt and the pepper. Immediately deglaze the whole casserole with still water and use a wooden spatula to remove the juices from the bottom of the casserole.

5 • Bring to a simmer. Continue cooking at low temperature for 4 hours while skimming regularly to remove any excess.

6 • At the end of the cooking time, strain the contents of the pot through a cheesecloth to recover only the essence. Your beef broth is ready!

Tip: To make a glaze or a demi-glace, reduce the broth while continuing to cook on high heat. Don't hesitate to transfer the contents of your pot into smaller and smaller pans as the broth reduces, to help it reduce down to a concentrate.

Vegetable peel broth

PREPARATION TIME: *2 min* – COOKING TIME: *1h 30*

1 • There are no ingredient lists for this recipe, but here's a tip:
as you cook, remember to store the peels of onions, garlic, carrots,
leek greens and roots, and spring onions the skin of ginger, the pods
of peas, edamame, etc. in an airtight bag in the refrigerator.

2 • Note: all the stems or flowers are not consumed: please make sure
to check if the trimmings, peels or leaves that you wish
to consume are edible.

3 • Place them in a pot of water.
Heat over medium heat for 1.5 hours to concentrate the flavors.

Fish broth
(FISH FUMET)

PREPARATION TIME: *20 min* – COOKING TIME: *40 min*

Ingredients

2 onions
2 leeks
1 stalk of celery
14 ounces (400 g) of fish trimmings and bones (from your fishmonger)
⅓ cup + 1½ tbsp. (100 ml) of mirin
4½ (1 litres) of water
1 bouquet garni
3½ tbsp. (50 g) soft butter
Grape seed oil

1 • Peel the onions and chop them finely. Rinse the leeks and celery and cut them into small cubes.

2 • In a casserole dish, heat a drizzle of olive oil and butter over medium heat. Once the butter has melted,
add the fish trimmings and bones. Fry for 1 minute and then add the shallots, onions, leeks and celery.
Fry for 1 more minute before adding the mirin. Mix well and add water to the top. Add the bouquet garni,
cover and cook over low heat for 35 minutes. Skim regularly.

3 • At the end of cooking, filter the contents of the casserole to keep only the clear juice of the fish stock.

*Tip: You can use this delicious broth for cooking and sauces
for dishes with a seafood flavor.*

Poultry stock

PREPARATION TIME: 20 min – COOKING TIME: 4 h 15

Ingredients

4.4 pounds (2 kg) of poultry or rabbit carcass
1 clove of garlic
2 shallots
8½ cups (2 litres) of water
1 bouquet garni (thyme and bay leaf in a green leek leaf)
1 sprig of rosemary
2 juniper berries
1 pinch of cracked pepper
scant ½ cup (100ml) grape seed oil
3½ tbsp. (50 g) of soft butter

1 • Crush the carcass and brown it in a stewpot with the grape seed oil and butter. Stir and simmer over medium heat until the carcass is a golden color. Remove it and set aside.

2 • Preheat the oven to 300°F (150°C /Gas Mark 2). Collect the fat in the stewpot with a small skimmer, keeping the juices at the bottom. Stew the garlic and shallots in these juices for about 5 minutes over medium heat. Remove from heat.

3 • Pour the water and add the bouquet garni before putting in the oven for 4 hours of cooking. 30 minutes before the end of the cooking time, add the sprig of rosemary, the juniper and the cracked pepper, and put it in the oven again.

4 • This infusion will serve to give power and taste to your stock. At the end of the 4 hours of cooking, filter the contents of the pot to keep only the juice and reserve it.

Vegetable broth

PREPARATION TIME: 5 min
COOKING TIME: 2 h
REST TIME: 30 min

Ingredients

4 carrots, diced
1 white leek
½ stalk celery
1 onion
1 bouquet garni
1 shallot
8½ cups (2 litres) of water
⅔ cup (150 ml) of white wine
1 star anise
3 cardamoms

1 • Dice the carrots.

2 • Put all the ingredients in a pot and simmer them for 2 hours, covered.

3 • Leave to stand for 30 minutes off the heat, then strain the broth.

Rice

In the recipes of this book, there is an important ingredient,
primordial in Asian cuisine, sacred in Japanese cuisine and that is the basis
of the diet of billions of people… I'm talking about rice of course!

In the West, we use several varieties of rice: risotto rice, Camargue rice, long-grain rice,
basmati rice, and Thai rice. Connoisseurs know that these are not the only a few
commercial names and that there are in fact many varieties of rice.

The arrival of rice in Japan dates back several thousand years. For centuries, it was an
external sign of wealth and its cultivation and possession was reserved for the elite and
warriors. The peasants paid their taxes in rice. It is from the Edo era onwards that rice
culture became more accessible and open to the people, so that everyone could have rice
at their table. The knowledge and respect for rice culture in Japan has been in the DNA
of the Japanese for hundreds of years and one could write many books on all that one
should know about rice. Take an interest in this fabulous ingredient
that we don't know enough about in our western culture.

Today, there are over 150 varieties of rice grown in Japan, with quality standards
set by the Japanese Grain Control Agency. Among all these varieties, one is regularly
rated higher and used more than the others: koshihikari rice.

This shiny, short-grained, light rice can be used for many dishes,
from Japanese curries to simple bowls of hot rice, as well as sushi or, more classically,
your blanquette de veau, veal marengo or stuffed tomatoes!

Some information to better know and prepare your Japanese rice:

• To be light and slightly sticky, the rice must be rinsed: place the rice in a or a large
mixing bowl and immerse it in a large amount of water. Rub it in the water between
your fingers and in your palm. Drain it and repeat the process 3 to 5 times.

• One of the secrets to perfect rice texture is to let it soak for at least 30 minutes
before cooking it in a pot or rice cooker.

• The derivatives of rice in Japanese cuisine are numerous: sake is made from it,
but also vinegar, syrup, and mochi!

Basic Recipes

Homemade ketchup

SERVES *1 small bottle* – PREPARATION TIME: *10 min* – COOKING TIME: *30 min*

Ingredients

1 clove of garlic
1 red onion
6 ripe tomatoes
2 pinches of ground cumin
2 pinches of ground ginger
2 tbsp. tomato paste
2 tbsp. (20 g) brown sugar
scant ½ cup (100 ml) of red wine vinegar
2 tbsp. olive oil
salt, ground pepper

1 • Prepare the vegetables: peel the garlic and onion chop them finely. Peel the tomatoes and cut them into large pieces. Set them aside.

2 • In a saucepan, heat the olive oil over medium heat. Add the garlic and onion and sauté for 3 minutes. Sprinkle with cumin and ground ginger and stir in and stir in the tomato paste. Using a wooden spoon, mix well and add the crushed tomatoes. Mix and add the brown sugar. Bring to a boil, then simmer over low heat, covered, for 15 minutes, then uncovered for another 10 minutes, so that the mixture reduces. Add the wine vinegar and season with salt and pepper.

3 • Using a hand blender, blend the mixture for 2 minutes and strain through a sieve. Let it cool down before bottling.

Sakura denbu

SERVES *75 g* – PREPARATION TIME: *10 min* – COOKING TIME: 11 TO *14 min*

Japanese delicacy par excellence, sakura denbu is a fish crumble. The dish is colored to obtain the shade of the Japanese cherry blossom. It is easily found in Asian grocery stores or grocery stores specializing in Japanese products. Here's how to make it at home!

Ingredients

3½ ounces (100 g) of cod fillet
1 tbsp.+ 1 tsp. mirin
1 drop of food coloring
(red, cherry or pink)

1 • Place the cod on a small plate. Season it with the tablespoon of mirin and place the plate in the microwave for 1 minute.

2 • Using a fork, coarsely crumble the fish and place in a kitchen towel. Tighten the cloth around the fish, fold it and squeeze it so that the fish forms a firm ball. Place the cloth under a stream of cold water and rub the ball vigorously to crumble the fish into small peices. Squeeze out the water.

3 • Heat a skillet over medium heat and dry the fish for 8 minutes without stopping to stir. Use chopsticks for more efficiency.

4 • Add the teaspoon of mirin and the food coloring and cook while stirring for another 2 to 5 minutes. Your mixture should be pink and steamy.

Utensils

Kitchen chopsticks

Perfect utensil for handling food without damaging it. I have been cooking for many years using chopsticks, as does Chef Thierry Marx, for example.

Rice cooker

If there is an essential utensil in Japan, it is this one. The rice cooker is literally used to prepare rice but can also be used as a steamer. There are all types with various features.

Chef's knife

An 8–12-inch (20–30-cm) long, thick blade knife used for chopping, mincing and mincing.

Japanese mandolin

The Japanese mandolin is a utensil with interchangeable blades used to slice food more or less finely.

Steamer basket

A cooking utensil easily found in Asian grocery stores or online that allows you to steam any ingredient by placing it on a basket over a large volume of boiling water.

Japanese frying pan

The pan to use when you want to make Japanese omelettes!

Nabe

Pot or cauldron in Japanese. The word designates both the container and the dishes prepared in it.

Wok

Necessary for cooking vegetables or stir-frying soba, for example.

The Different

Paring knife

3–4 inches (7–10cm) long, with a thick, short and very sharp blade. It is used to peel, remove stalks and make small cuts.

Chef's knife

8–12 inches (20–30 cm) long, with a thick blade, used for chopping, chiseling, slicing. It is the most common and versatile tool in any kitchen.

Fillet of sole

6–8 inches (15–22cm) long, with a very thin blade, useful for lifting fish fillets.

Knives

Santoku with honeycomb blade

Japanese version of the chef's knife, it has a honeycombed blade: the honeycomb creates air cushions that prevent food from sticking to the blade.

Mushroom knife

This small knife with a curved blade is perfect for picking mushrooms and cutting them clean without damaging them.

Bread knife

A long knife with a serrated blade, it is perfect for cutting foods with a thin skin or a thick crust.

Baking Basics

Sesame Potato Bun

SERVES *4 buns*
PREPARATION TIME: *20 min*
REST TIME: *1 hour and 20 minutes*
COOKING TIME: *20 min*

Ingredients

1 mashed potato
1 packet of baking powder
Scant 1 cup (200 ml) warm milk
2½ cups (340 g) flour type 55
1 tsp. (6 g) salt
1 tsp. (6 g) sugar
3½ tbsp. (55 g) butter
in pieces
1 egg yolk

1 • Prepare the mashed potatoes: peel the potatoes and steam them in a steamer basket, or boil in a pot of water. Drain it once it is cooked through and use a potato masher and a fine sieve to obtain a fine pulp.

2 • Pour the baker's yeast into the warm milk and stir. Let the mixture ferment for 5 minutes.

3 • Place and mix the potato pulp, flour, yeast, salt and sugar in the bowl of a food processor fitted with a dough hook. Add the yeast milk and mix on medium speed for 2 to 3 minutes until smooth.

4 • Add the butter to the bowl of the food processor and pulse for an additional 7 minutes, until the dough is smooth and shiny. Cover the dough with a tea towel and let it develop for 45 min.

5 • Flour your work surface: place the dough on it, remove excess air from the dough and separate it into 4 equal pieces. Shape them into balls. Cover them again and let them rest and expand for another 30 minutes.

6 • Preheat the oven to 356°F (180 °C Gas Mark 4). Brush with egg yolks and sprinkle with sesame seeds before baking for 20 minutes.

Butter Brioche

SERVES 4 – PREPARATION TIME: 20 min

RESTING TIME: 4 h – COOKING TIME: 20 min

Ingredients

1 cup (125 g) of flour type 45	2 tbsp. (20 g) powdered sugar
1 level tsp. of dry yeast	1 pinch of salt
1 whole egg + 4 yolks	Scant ⅓ cup (80 g) soft butter

1 • In the bowl of a food processor, pour the flour, yeast, whole egg and 3 egg yolks. Add the sugar and a pinch of salt and beat at medium speed for 5 minutes. Add the soft butter and beat for another 10 minutes.

2 • Flour a round-bottomed mixing bowl and place the dough in it. Filter and let it grow for 1 hour.

3 • Flour the work surface. Place the brioche dough on top. Expel the excess air from the dough with your fist and knead it for a few moments before wrapping it again and placing it in the refrigerator for at least 2 hours.

4 • Once this time has elapsed, take the dough out of the refrigerator and let it come to room temperature. Then press it with your fist to release the gas and cut it into 8 equal balls. Butter or grease a brioche pan and place the dough balls in it, one next to the other.

5 • Set aside at room temperature for an additional 1 hour.

6 • Preheat oven to 356°F (180°C / gas mark 6). Mix the remaining egg yolk with a little water and, using a brush, brush on the brioche before putting it in the oven for 20 minutes.

Homemade bread loaf

SERVES *1 loaf of bread* – PREPARATION TIME: *20 min* – REST TIME: *1 h*
COOKING TIME: *30 min*

Ingredients

2¼ tbsp. (40 g) butter
3⅓ cups (400 g) flour type 45
2 tbsp. (15 g) powdered sugar
1½ tsp. (8 g) fine salt
1 tbsp. (16 g) fresh baker's yeast
⅔ cup (150 ml) warm milk
½ cup (80 ml) of water

1 • Preheat oven to 86°F(30°C / Gas Mark 1). In a small saucepan, melt the butter
and remove from heat.

2 • Prepare the bread dough: pour the flour, sugar and salt into the bowl of a food processor
fitted with a dough hook. Mix well. Crumble the yeast and add it to the dry ingredients.
Add the warm milk and water and knead at slow speed for 2 to 3 minutes. Add the melted
butter and knead on medium speed for 8 to 10 minutes.

3 • Once your dough is smooth, transfer it to a baking dish. Cover with a clean cloth
and place the pan on the oven door. The gentle, indirect heat will allow the dough
to develop. Let it grow for 30 minutes.

4 • Lightly flour your hands and work surface. After the first resting period, expel excess air
from the dough with your fist, then place it on your work surface and knead it for 1 minute
to give it strength. Make a dough piece and put it in the loaf pan. Close the pan three quarters
of the way and let the dough rest for another 30 minutes.

5 • Preheat oven to 392°F (200°C / Gas Mark 6). Close the pan completely. Put in the oven and
lower the temperature to 356°F (180 °C / Gas Mark 4). Bake for 45 minutes.

6 • Turn the bread out onto a rack as soon as it is done baking. Wait until it has reached
room temperature before cutting and eating it.

Shortcrust pastry

1 • Place the flour and salt in a mixing bowl. Mix well and add the butter in pieces. Knead the whole for 2 minutes by hand and then sand the mix between your fingers.

2 • Pour in the ice water at once to create a thermal shock and knead again for 1 minute, until it forms a smooth ball.

3 • Clingfilm and place the dough in the refrigerator for 2 hours.

4 • Your shortcrust pastry is ready to use.

SERVES *250 g* OF DOUGH
PREPARATION TIME: *10 min*
REST TIME: *2 h*

Ingredients

2 cups (250 g) of flour
⅓ cup (125 g) cold butter
½ cup (125 ml) very cold water
1 tbsp. (5 g) salt

Anko paste

SERVES *350 g* OF DOUGH — PREPARATION TIME: *10 min* — REST TIME: *2 h* — COOKING TIME: *1 h 15*

1 • Soak the azuki beans for 2 hours in a container of cold water.

2 • Drain and place in a saucepan. Cover them with water and bring to a boil. Let cook at a low boil for 5 minutes. Drain the beans and repeat the process, changing the water.

3 • Once the beans are blanched and free of any bitterness, pour the mineral water into the pot and immerse the beans. Cook them at a low boil for 50 minutes to 1 hour, until they are soft in the middle.

4 • Remove from heat and leave in the water for an additional 10 minutes.

5 • Remove a third of the cooking water, add the sugar and a pinch of salt. Over medium heat, resume cooking and simmer for another 15 to 20 minutes, stirring regularly. The idea is to let the mixture reduce to a nice purée, not too liquid but slightly syrupy. Your paste is ready!

Ingredients

1 cup (200 g) azuki beans
Scant 3 cups (700 ml) mineral water
¾ cup (180 g) sugar
1 pinch of salt

SERVES *1 cake of 4 parts*
PREPARATION TIME: *10 min* – REST TIME: *1 h*

Ingredients

5 gelatin sheets
1 cup (200 g) sugar
Scant ½ cup (100 ml) water
1 cup (200 g) glucose or isomalt
7 ounces (200 g) dark chocolate
½ cup (135 g) unsweetened condensed milk

Chocolate Frosting

1 • Dip the gelatin sheets in a bowl of cold water and set aside for a few moments.

2 • Make a sugar syrup: pour the sugar, water and glucose into a saucepan. Bring to a boil and stop cooking once the sugar reaches 221°F (105°C).

3 • Place the chocolate in a bowl and pour the syrup over it. Add the condensed milk. Drain the gelatin leaves and squeeze out the excess water. Place them in the bowl with the chocolate, syrup and milk.

4 • Using an immersion blender, blend the mixture for 30 seconds: place the mixer at the bottom of your container and not on the surface of the mixture to avoid letting air into the mixture. Your frosting is almost ready, wait until it has come down to a temperature of 90°F (32°C) to use it.

5 • Finally, as with the chocolate icing, place your cake on a wire rack, and place it on a baking sheet. Use a ladle to pour the glaze from the center of the cake. Pour generously so that the cake is perfectly covered. Place in the refrigerator for 1 hour to allow the glaze to set.

Kiki's Delivery Service

You can photocopy this page to cut out the stencil shapes!

Green

Red

White

White

KIKI

Soy sauce

If rice is a basic ingredient of the Japanese diet, the same is obviously true for soy sauce, which is sometimes used as a simple seasoning sauce, sometimes as a basic ingredient for marinades or as a cooking stock.

Like many ingredients used in Japan, soy sauce originated in China. There are different versions and ways of making it depending on its country of origin. We will focus on Japanese soy sauce.

In Japan, soy sauce is made by fermenting soybeans and wheat. Koji is used as a ferment but also salt, which serves as a preservative.

We can distinguish 3 types of soy sauce:

• Classic soy sauce, also known as dark soy sauce, is the best known and the one you probably have at home.

• The clear soy sauce is less used, it is certainly clearer but also more salty.

• Soy sauce called tamari, which has very little or no wheat content. It is the darkest sauce and its taste is more pronounced. If you are allergic to gluten, this soy sauce is for you because, under this name, you will only find sauces prepared exclusively with soy.

There are many brands of soy sauce and many manufacturers whose flavors and know-how are very particular. Traditionally, the fermentation and production of soy sauce takes place over many weeks or even months. Naturally fermented, soy sauces have deep, sometimes complex flavors and are part of the umami, the 5th flavor, the very special taste of Japanese cuisine.

In supermarkets or in large-scale distribution, you will easily find soy sauce. Be aware that it is usually produced chemically by hydrolysis and addition of other ingredients in order to reduce considerably its production time. It goes from several months to only a few days. No need to specify that its taste is not as developed on the aromatic level.

Some uses of soy sauce that will change your daily life:

• Use it to season meats, deglaze casseroles or pans, or simply season rice. Use it to replace salt. You can also use it in less salty versions.

• Use it to make your *ajitsuke tamago*, the ramen eggs: after cooking the eggs in boiling water for 6 min, plunge them in ice water and shell them. Then dip them in a bath of soy sauce and let them marinate for at least 30 min and up to 24 h in the refrigerator. It's as simple as that and it's a nice change from hard-boiled eggs. Here you are with a pure bite of umami and Japan!

• When marinating eggs, tofu or meat, soy sauce is the main ingredient of the marinade, so it is important to use good quality soy sauce. There are all types and prices available: don't hesitate to choose quality when possible, your cooking and tasting experience will be enhanced!

ヤマサ 上

本醸造
特選

有機しょうゆ

大地の恵みの有機栽培の大豆と小麦、
海の恵みの天日塩で仕込みました。

ECOCERT

自然からの
贈り物

500ml

Seasonings

Cooking Sake

Although used in the same way as mirin, it is less sweet than mirin. It is quite different from brewed sake designed for consumption and is an indispensable ingredient for anyone who wants to cook Japanese food.

Organic soy sauce

Salty amber sauce made from soy and wheat. It is used for seasoning or marinating foods. There are several types of soy sauce. It takes its name from the hishio paste, originally made from a marinade of fish and meat mixed with soy and wheat. Now widespread, this sauce can be found in many supermarkets.

Mirin

Yellow and syrupy liquid, quite similar to a very sweet sake. It is used as a seasoning in Japanese or Korean cuisine, in marinades, in sauces or in cooking.

and Sauces

Black sesame oil

Another classic of Japanese and Asian cuisine, black sesame oil is an oil with a strong aroma of roasted sesame. It is used to season dishes or marinades.

Ponzu sauce

A mixture of soy sauce and Japanese citrus juice. It is used in the same way as soy sauce.

Yuzu juice

In cooking, it is always interesting to be able to work with fruit, and use the acidity to counteract the fat and the sweetness in the mouth. Yuzu juice is a must have when you want to cook Japanese. Yuzu is a citrus fruit native to Asia, with a thick and bumpy skin. A hybrid of lemon and tangerine, it has a very distinctive (and fabulous) tart taste. You can use its juice and zest as you would a lemon.

Index

Acknowledgements

I am so happy to have been able to create this book, I have been dreaming about it for years and it is thanks to your support and trust that I was able to finally make it. Thank you from the bottom of my heart.

Thank you to Bérengère for having made me discover, a few years ago now, all the work of Studio Ghibli. Thank you for all the passion and talent with which you designed this book. I am so happy that we could finally propose our vision of the Ghibli recipes with this book!

Henri, you already know well the adventures of *Kiki's Delivery Service*, I am so excited that we can finally discover the other heroes and heroines of the works of Miyazaki and Takahata!

Thank you to my parents and my sister for their unwavering support, love and trust.

Thank you to Judith and Nicolas who, through their passion and professionalism, have brought my recipes to life! Nicolas, we have been working together for several years now and I think we have built a bond and a trust that I am proud of.

Thank you to my team and especially to Baptiste who is a trusted right-hand man who allows me to create with freedom and serenity.

Thanks to all the people who helped me to realize this book, by their advice, their loans, their time.

Thank you to Antoine, Fannie and the entire team at Café Bleu in Chartres: your restaurant is a place of life, sharing and passion, from which it was a pleasure to write the recipes for this book.

Thanks to Catherine, Antoine and Anne from Hachette Heroes for the trust they have put in me for several years now. It is always an honor and a pleasure to work with you. Thank you for believing in me and my project. Anne, thank you for being such an understanding, open-minded, and passionate editor. Thank you for your patience with me, I know I am not easy to work with at times.

Thank you to all the teams at Hachette Heroes who will bring this book to you and give it the light it deserves.

A final and big thank you to my dear community, readers, viewers, fans of the first hour or spectators of the shadow. Thank you. Thank you. Thank you.

Butter is happiness,

Thibaud Villanova
Gastronogeek

© 2022, Hachette Livre (Hachette Pratique).
58, rue Jean Bleuzen – 92178 Vanves Cedex

For the publisher, the principle is to use papers made of natural, renewable, recyclable fibers and manufactured from wood from forests that adopt a sustainable management system. In addition, the publisher expects its paper suppliers to be part of a recognized environmental certification process.

Management: Catherine Saunier-Talec

Project manager: Antoine Béon

Project manager: Anne Vallet

Design and illustrations: Bérengère Demoncy

Proofreading: Charlotte Buch-Müller

Production: Anne-Laure Soyez

Background credits: Adobe Stock: rrice, siam4510, tota, 背景屋

«Studio Ghibli» and the titles of the studio's films are trademarks of Kabushiki Kaisha Studio Ghibli.
The book *The Unofficial Ghibli Cookbook* is in no way an official Studio Ghibli book, nor validated by Studio Ghibli. No official illustrations or film clips have been used in the making of this book. It is a book of recipes created by fans of Studio Ghibli's works, none of them working or being affiliated with Studio Ghibli. This book, whose author is Thibaud VIllanova, is written for pedagogical, informational and cultural purposes.

Castle in the Sky is a film by Hayao Miyazaki
My Neighbor Totoro is a film by Hayao Miyazaki
Kiki's Delivery Service is a film by Hayao Miyazaki
Only Yesterday is a film by Isao Takahata
Porco Rosso is a film by Hayao Miyazaki
Pom Poko is a film by Isao Takahata
Whisper of the Heart is a film by Yoshifumi Kondō
Princess Mononoke is a film by Hayao Miyazaki
My Neighbors the Yamadas is a film by Isao Takahata

Spirited Away is a film by Hayao Miyazaki
The Cat Returns is a film by Hiroyuki Morita
Howl's Moving Castle is a film by Hayao Miyazaki
Tales from Earthsea is a film by Gorō Miyazaki *Ponyo* is a film by Hayao Miyazaki
The Secret World of Arrietty is a film by Hiromasa Yonebayashi
From Up on Poppy Hill is a film by Gorō Miyazaki
The Wind Rises is a film by Hayao Miyazaki
When Marnie Was There is a film by Hiromasa Yonebayashi
Earwig and the Witch is a film by Gorō Miyazaki

Printed in China by Toppan
WWW.GASTRONOGEEK.COM

Published by Titan Books, London, in 2022.

TITAN
BOOKS

A division of Titan Publishing Group Ltd
144 Southwark Street
London SE1 0UP
www.titanbooks.com

Find us on Facebook: www.facebook.com/titanbooks
Follow us on Twitter: @TitanBooks

Published by arrangement with Hachette Heroes:
www.hachetteheroes.com

A CIP catalogue record for this title is available from the British Library.
ISBN: 9781803363523